Homepages.Maths.Year 5

Robin Grist, Philippa Hepworth,
Jackie Cook, Veronica Parker and
Mike Spooner

Published in 2001 by
Nelson Thornes Limited
Delta Place
27 Bath Road
Cheltenham
GL53 7TH
United Kingdom

01 02 03 04 05 \ 10 9 8 7 6 5 4 3 2 1

A catalogue record for this book is available from the British Library

ISBN 0-7487-5674-4

Illustrations by Uwe Mayer, David Mostyn and Andy Peters
Page make-up by Aetos Ltd

Printed and bound in Great Britain by Bath Press

This publication contains material from the National Numeracy Strategy, produced by the Department for Education and Employment. © Crown copyright. Reproduced under the terms of HMSO Guidance Note 8.

Contents

Introduction

Homepages.Maths offers a series of homework activities written to develop and improve the numeracy skills of children in Year 5. The tasks are directly linked to the National Numeracy Strategy. The activities are designed to support and complement the work of the class teacher, enabling pupils to have additional practice, particularly in developing their mental facility and supporting the development of independent learning.

In Year 5, at least two activities for each week of the school year are provided. These activities include the use of the home context, number games and puzzles, problems and short written exercises and tasks. In addition, there are six mental mathematics quizzes and nine mathematics language quizzes designed to be used regularly throughout the year.

It is intended that with all of these activities, parents, guardians or another adult should be involved directly, sharing the activities and enhancing the child–parent–teacher partnership.

Some of the key features of the 'Homepages' programme include:
- The tasks are easy to administer through the use of photocopiable resource sheets.
- Emphasis is placed on developing pupils' understanding of everyday mathematical vocabulary. The mental maths and language quizzes, in particular, provide opportunities for children to use and extend their mathematical language.
- The activities are designed to be both enjoyable and meaningful.
- Some of the games identified within the activities can be played on a regular basis – not just over the course of one week. They enable children to practise and reinforce skills in different situations and should contribute towards a greater understanding and enjoyment of maths on the part of both parents and children.
- The activities are intended to be completed in approximately 15 to 20 minutes, but can be extended if time and the children's enthusiasm allows.
- Most of the activities do not require the teacher to mark the pupils' work. Those requiring marking will take very little time.
- Emphasis has been placed on supporting the work that has already taken place in the classroom.
- Advice and guidance to parents on the operation of each activity and how they might support their child is included. Instructions to pupils and parents have deliberately been kept to a minimum and are designed to be clear and unambiguous.
- The pupils are able to keep a record of activities they have done by completing their own record of achievement (see page xv for photocopiable recording sheet).

On-line support

In addition to the materials provided in each 'Homepages' title, on-line support is provided on our web site. Visit the web site at www.nelsonthornes.com.

Glossary

A list of mathematical vocabulary that children need to understand and use in Year 5 is provided for parents, who are encouraged to use these words and phrases as they arise in the home environment. Parents or other adults can also be encouraged to use these words in discussions with their children and to listen for children using these words fluently and correctly.

Additional resources for parents and children

In addition to a pencil and paper the activities make use of household items in everyday use.

To carry out all the activities within this book, the following items would also be useful:

- A pack of playing cards
- Two sets of coloured counters – 15 of each
- 1 die with numbers 1 to 6
- 1 blank six-sided die on which the parents can write with a felt pen
- A few sheets of squared paper
- A ruler
- Sheets of thin card
- A mirror
- A pair of scissors
- Glue

It is recommended that schools inform parents about these additional items before any of the resource sheets are sent home. Alternatively, the school might provide a pack of these items at very low cost.

Medium-term planning

The termly planners on pages viii to xiv show how the 'Homepages' activities can be linked to the *Framework for Teaching Mathematics*. This planner offers a starting point from which you can build your own homework plans.

The mental maths and language quizzes are designed to be repeated regularly throughout the year. Some of the games might also be played on a regular basis – not just over the course of a week.

With all of this in mind a template version of the termly planner has been provided on the web site, enabling teachers to develop their own plans to meet the needs of their pupils.

Key to a Homepages resource sheet

List of resources and preparatory notes for each activity

Symbol indicates nature and purpose of activity as follows:

written exercises intended to be worked on independently, although there is scope for parental support

games that parents (or another adult) and children work on together

number puzzles that develop the children's problem-solving skills

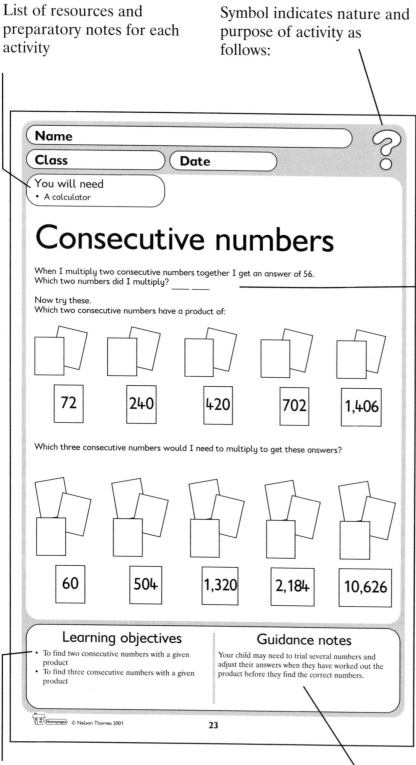

Name

Class   **Date**

You will need
• A calculator

Consecutive numbers

When I multiply two consecutive numbers together I get an answer of 56.
Which two numbers did I multiply? ___ ___

Now try these.
Which two consecutive numbers have a product of:

| 72 | 240 | 420 | 702 | 1,406 |

Which three consecutive numbers would I need to multiply to get these answers?

| 60 | 504 | 1,320 | 2,184 | 10,626 |

Learning objectives
• To find two consecutive numbers with a given product
• To find three consecutive numbers with a given product

Guidance notes
Your child may need to trial several numbers and adjust their answers when they have worked out the product before they find the correct numbers.

Homepages © Nelson Thornes 2001   23

activities that make use of the home context, allowing children to consolidate skills in different contexts

mental maths and language quizzes allow children to consolidate mental strategies and use important mathematical language. They allow children to talk about maths with their parents

Where detailed instructions are given, for a game or puzzle for example, then it is intended that an adult should read these to the child

Objective for the week's activity linked to *Framework for Teaching Mathematics* termly planning (see page viii for planning framework).

Guidance notes offer advice and support to parents or other adults when carrying out the activity with a child

Dear Parent/Guardian

Homepages.Maths is a new series of homework activities written to develop and improve the numeracy skills of your child in Year 5. The activities are designed to support and complement the work your child will be doing at school, particularly in developing his or her mental mathematical skills.

For the activities to be a success, it is essential that you work with and support your child in all of them. You will need a limited number of resources from your home to assist with the activities in addition to a very small list of items of equipment that we are able to provide at a minimal cost.

The activities include two sets of quizzes to be used on a regular basis throughout the year. In all of these you will need to read the questions to your child and help him or her with any he or she finds particularly difficult.

Considerable emphasis is placed on the use of mathematical games and it is important you play them with your child and explain the rules. Children enjoy playing games and the ones we provide you with can be used on a regular basis, not only during the week they are sent home. The games are particularly valuable in giving your child additional practice and reinforcing skills he or she has developed at school. With the other activities your child may need help to see where to write the answers, and in all activities it is important your child enjoys them and does not feel threatened or concerned about any they find difficult. We have included some guidance notes to assist you with each activity.

In developing your child's understanding of mathematics there are a large number of words and phrases that he or she will need to know. We have provided a list of many of those that are likely to be new, and would encourage you to use them, at the appropriate times, in the home environment.

The time your child is expected to spend on each activity should not be more than 15 to 20 minutes – for many children it will be less. However, you may decide to continue beyond this time – if you are playing a game, for example.

Your child will bring home at least one activity each week, with the quizzes offering additional challenges over the course of each term. If at any time you have any particular concerns we would like to hear from you.

Finally, we have included a record of achievement for your child to fill in when he or she has completed each activity. These sheets should build into a comprehensive record of your child's progress.

Regards

Homepages.Maths termly planning sheets

Autumn term

Week	Topic	Homepages.Maths activity	Learning objectives
1	Solving problems and finding answers in words in a word search.	A mathematical word search.	Accurate +, −, ×, ÷ of whole numbers and fractions. Solving problems.
	A number puzzle.	Empty boxes.	To use +, − to solve number puzzles.
2	Using a multiplication grid.	27 mistakes.	Accurate recall of multiplication facts up to 10×10.
	Using a simple code.	How big is your name?	Solving problems. Quick and accurate addition of one- and two-digit numbers.
3	Four rules of number.	Number search.	To know addition facts and corresponding subtraction facts. Also division and corresponding multiplication facts.
	A number puzzle.	Making numbers.	Accurate +, −, ×, ÷ of whole numbers and fractions. To order numbers including negative numbers.
4	Money problems.	Make 50p.	To solve money problems using coins up to 20p.
	Finding pairs of numbers incorrectly added on a grid.	A difference square.	Quick and accurate subtraction of pairs of one- and two-digit numbers.
5	Reasoning about shapes and recognising them according to their properties.	Is it the same shape?	To be able to recognise and name 2D shapes.
	A card game using mental strategies of addition.	Adding to 27.	Quick and accurate recall of addition of sets of two or more numbers.
6	Estimating and measuring accurately in cm and mm.	Estimating and measuring 1	To be able to estimate the height, width, or length of an object in mm and cm.
	Using number chains to practise mental arithmetic skills.	Number chains.	Accurately following a series of instructions involving +, −, ×, ÷ of whole numbers and fractions.
7	Describing and visualising 3D shapes.	Guess the shape.	To be able to classify 3D shapes by knowing their properties. To recognise an octahedron.
	A game that requires a strategy for achieving the highest possible total of three numbers.	Make it big.	To develop a game strategy; quick and accurate addition of two-digit numbers.

Week	Topic	Homepages.Maths activity	Learning objectives
8	Measuring and estimating using cm and m.	Estimating and measuring 2.	To estimate and check the height, width or length of objects in cm and m.
	Using a dart board to find different combinations of numbers totalling 50.	Dart to 50.	Quick and accurate addition of 3 numbers totalling 50. Developing a systematic approach.
9	Using co-ordinates to draw different 2D shapes.	Shape up.	To read and plot co-ordinates in the first quadrant. Naming 2D shapes.
	Completing number sentences using a given list of numbers.	Take two.	Addition and subtraction of two two-digit numbers. Finding a strategy.
10	Solving number puzzles.	Two missing numbers.	To solve number puzzles using the four rules of number.
	A puzzle to make 88 using the digits 1 to 8.	Making 88.	Developing a strategy. Quick and accurate +, − of one- and two-digit numbers.
11	Solving number puzzles.	Number puzzles.	To solve number puzzles using the four rules of number.
	A cross number puzzle using the four rules of number and fractions.	Cross number puzzle.	To solve problems using the four rules of number. To find simple fractional quantities and to round up/down numbers.
12	Multiplying consecutive numbers.	Consecutive numbers.	To find pairs of consecutive numbers, or groups of three consecutive numbers with a given product.
	Completing number sentences by choosing from a set of numbers to make different target numbers.	Hitting the target.	To develop a strategy. Addition and subtraction of three two-digit numbers.
13	Solving money problems.	Smallest amount of coins.	To be able to solve problems involving money.
	Completing addition and subtraction questions with missing digits,	Mind the gap.	To reason and solve number problems involving +, − of two- and three-digit numbers.
14	Shape and space – recognising the perpendicular.	Perpendicular.	To know that perpendicular lines are at right angles to each other and to recognise them in the environment.
	Finding mistakes in a completed addition square.	An addition square.	Quick and accurate addition of pairs of one- and two-digit numbers.

Homepages.Maths termly planning sheets

Spring term

Week	Topic	Homepages.Maths activity	Learning objectives
1	Shape and space – recognising the word parallel and objects that have parallel edges.	Parallel.	To know that parallel lines are same distance apart and to recognise them in the environment.
	Solving problems and finding answers in words in a word search.	A mathematical word search.	Accurate +, −, ×, ÷ of whole numbers. To solve problems involving money, time and length.
2	Finding the areas of rectangles in cm².	Finding areas.	To be able to measure and calculate the area of rectangles in cm using the formula.
	Using number chains to practise mental arithmetic skills.	Number chains.	Accurately following a series of instructions involving +, doubling, ÷ and fractions.
3	Addition and multiplication grids.	Fill the gaps.	Quick recall of addition and multiplication facts.
	A game that requires a strategy for making a given total.	Making 100.	To develop a game strategy; quick and accurate addition of two-digit numbers.
4	Adding fractions.	Fraction triangles.	To add fractions using whole numbers, halves and quarters.
	A number puzzle.	Making numbers.	To +, −, ×, ÷ one- and two-digit numbers. To order numbers including negative numbers and fractions.
5	Line symmetry.	Symmetry.	To recognise lines of symmetry.
	A puzzle to make 99 using the digits 1 to 9.	Making 99.	Developing a strategy to +, − one- and two-digit numbers.
6	Accurate measurement and calculation of perimeters.	Measure to the nearest millimetre.	To be able to measure to the nearest mm and to calculate perimeters.
	A game of bingo to reinforce table facts.	Bingo.	Quick and accurate recall of the 2 to 10 times tables.
7	Time	Travelling times.	To recall the time, use 24-hour clock notation and calculate units of time.
	Complete number sentences by choosing from a set of numbers to make different target numbers.	Hitting the target.	To develop a strategy. To add three two-digit numbers.

Week	Topic	Homepages.Maths activity	Learning objectives
8	Addition of groups of numbers.	Number routes.	To add strings of two- and three-digit numbers.
	A puzzle using the four fours.	4, 4, 4, 4	To +, −, ×, ÷ one- and two-digit numbers. To record in a systematic way.
9	Area – using formula to find areas of rectangles.	Finding smaller areas.	To use the formula and record it in words and letters. To calculate in mm².
	Number sequences.	Number sequences in a square.	To find patterns to complete number sequences – whole numbers and decimals.
10	Accurate measurement up to tenths of a litre – capacity.	Measuring in tenths of a litre.	To record in ml and tenths of a litre. To read a scale to the nearest $^1/_{10}$ litre.
	Using a dart board to find different combinations of numbers totalling 62.	Darting doubles.	Quick and accurate addition of three numbers totalling 62, including doubles. Developing a systematic approach.
11	Odd and even numbers.	Odds and evens.	To make general statements about odd and even numbers.
	A cross number puzzle using the four rules of number, and money.	A number puzzle.	To solve number and money problems using the four rules of number.
12	Time – using units of time and converting a.m./p.m. to 24-hour clock.	School timetable.	To be able to use 24-hour notation and to read a timetable.
	Completing addition and subtraction sums with missing digits.	Mind the gap.	To reason and solve +, − problems of two- and three-digit numbers.
13	Weighing to 100g units.	Measuring in tenths of a kilogram.	To record estimates and read a scale in tenths of a kg.
	A decimal number puzzle.	Decimal sums.	Quick and accurate addition of pairs of decimal numbers. Finding a strategy for eliminating pairs.

Homepages.Maths termly planning sheets

Summer term

Week	Topic	Homepages.Maths activity	Learning objectives
1	Temperature reading.	Daily temperatures.	To read temperature scales including positive and negative.
	A number puzzle.	Making numbers.	To +, −, ×, ÷ one- and two-digit numbers. To order numbers including fractions and negative numbers.
2	Data handling. Multiples of 2, 3 and 5.	Tree diagram.	To recognise multiples of 2, 3 and 5. To record data using a tree diagram.
	A number puzzle to find pairs of decimals incorrectly added.	A decimal addition square.	To add pairs of decimal numbers.
3	Addition and multiplication of numbers.	More grids.	To solve number puzzles using addition and multiplication facts.
	Solving fractional problems and finding answers in words in a word search.	A fractional word search.	To find fractional amounts of quantities involving weight, length, money and time.
4	Fractions.	Down and across.	To add fractions using whole numbers, halves, quarters, eighths and tenths.
	Using number chains to practise mental arithmetic skills.	Number chains.	To be able to accurately follow a series of instructions involving +, −, ×, ÷, decimals and fractions.
5	Data handling using tally charts and bar line charts.	Roll the dice.	To be able to test a hypothesis about the frequency of an event and draw a bar line chart.
	A number game that requires a strategy for making a given total.	Making 99	To develop a game strategy and to +, − two-digit numbers.
6	Probability.	What chance?	To discuss events and to know the likelihood of them happening. To sequence events according to the probability of them happening.
	A cross number puzzle requiring the solving of money problems.	A money puzzle.	To be able to solve money problems using four rules of number, fractions, decimals and percentages.

Week	Topic	Homepages.Maths activity	Learning objectives
7	Triangles and their properties.	Identify the shape.	To be able to identify different triangles and recognise scalene and congruent triangles.
	A decimal number puzzle.	Decimal differences.	To be able to add pairs of decimal numbers. To find a strategy for eliminating inappropriate pairs.
8	A number puzzle.	Making numbers.	To be able to +, −, ×, ÷ one- and two-digit numbers. To order numbers including fractions and negative numbers.
9	Symmetrical patterns.	Growing symmetry.	Recognise where a shape will be reflected into a mirror line parallel to one side.
	Number puzzles.	What's the number?	To solve simple word problems.
10	A cross number puzzle using the four rules of number to solve measurement problems.	A measurement puzzle.	To solve measurement problems involving capacity, length, mass and time.
11	Number puzzle using multiplying and dividing.	Number chains.	To recognise odd and even numbers and solve number puzzles.
12	A game involving factors of numbers to 100.	Factors, factors, factors.	To understand factors and to find factors of numbers to 100.
	Nets of a cube.	Which will make an open cube?	To be able to identify nets which will make an open cube.
13	Recognising acute, obtuse and right angles.	Which angle is it?	To be able to identify and draw acute and obtuse angles.

Homepages.Maths planning sheets

For quizzes

Topic	Homepages.Maths activity	Learning objectives
Money problems.	**Maths Language Quiz 1.**	To solve money problems.
Looking at graphs.	**Maths Language Quiz 2.**	To solve problems by interpreting data in graphs.
Square numbers.	**Maths Language Quiz 3.**	To recognise square numbers.
Decimal numbers.	**Maths Language Quiz 4.**	To order sets of decimal numbers and to round decimals to the nearest whole number.
Fractions.	**Maths Language Quiz 5.**	To find fractional amounts of numbers and money.
Shape – area and perimeter.	**Maths Language Quiz 6.**	To measure and calculate areas and perimeters of simple shapes.
Number – factors	**Maths Language Quiz 7.**	To identify the factors of numbers.
Percentages.	**Maths Language Quiz 8.**	To find percentages of numbers and money.
Number puzzles.	**Maths Language Quiz 9.**	To solve mathematical puzzles.
Various aspects of mathematics.	**Mental Maths Quizzes 1–6.**	To revise a range of mathematical topics.

Individual record sheet

Name | **Date**

Activity

Child's comments

I worked ...	Very well	☺	Quite hard	😐	Not very well	☹
I enjoyed this activity	A lot	☺	A little	😐	Not much	☹
I was helped	Not at all	☺	A little	😐	A lot	☹
I found this activity	Very easy	☺	About right	😐	Difficult	☹
I learned	A lot	☺	A little	😐	Not much	☹

Parent/carer's comments

My child found this activity ...	Easy	☺	About right	😐	Challenging	☹
My child needed ...	No help	☺	A little help	😐	A lot of help	☹

A mathematical word search

T	H	R	E	E	L	P	Z	E	N	Y	F	T	T
E	N	I	N	E	T	Y	F	I	V	E	O	H	N
E	I	G	H	T	Y	O	N	E	M	U	R	I	E
E	L	P	Q	E	R	T	Y	K	F	F	T	R	N
N	M	E	F	I	F	T	Y	S	I	X	Y	T	T
F	S	E	P	O	F	R	M	E	F	L	S	Y	Y
S	I	X	T	Y	T	W	O	V	T	Q	I	S	S
Y	N	M	K	H	S	Q	W	E	Y	B	X	I	I
K	Q	T	H	I	R	T	Y	N	O	C	X	X	M
Z	A	Q	S	O	I	R	X	Z	N	F	L	H	E
S	I	X	T	W	E	N	T	Y	F	O	U	R	V
Y	J	J	E	I	G	H	T	Y	N	R	N	E	Y
T	H	I	R	T	Y	E	I	G	H	T	P	G	Q
N	I	N	E	T	Y	J	E	V	E	Y	J	B	R

1. How many centimetres is $^1/_{100}$ of 3 metres? ....
2. .... − 52 = 29.
3. Three-quarters of 48 is ....
4. How many tickets at £8 can I buy if I have £58? ....
5. 102, 96, ..., 84.

6. Two-thirds of 60 equals ....
7. One quarter of 96 is ....
8. Double a number is 76. What is the number? ....
9. 18 + 19 + 19 = ...
10. Half of 190 is ....
11. If I have £5 and spend £4.38, how many pence have I left? ....

Find the answers to each of the questions above in the word search. The answers are written in words either horizontally or vertically. When you have found the word put a ring around it.

Learning objectives

- Addition, subtraction, multiplication and division of whole numbers
- Simple fractions
- Solving problems involving length and money

Guidance notes

Explain to your child what he or she has to do if unsure. When your child has finished, talk about the answers and link them to the words in the word search.

Name

Class   Date

You will need
• A pencil

Empty boxes

For each of the number statements below choose three numbers from 11, 7, 4 and 2 to make them correct.

$$\boxed{} + \boxed{} + \boxed{} = 17$$

$$\boxed{} - \boxed{} + \boxed{} = 14$$

$$\boxed{} + \boxed{} - \boxed{} = 13$$

$$\boxed{} + \boxed{} + \boxed{} = 13$$

$$\boxed{} - \boxed{} + \boxed{} = 9$$

$$\boxed{} + \boxed{} - \boxed{} = 0$$

For each of these number sentences choose three numbers from 9, 7, 4 and 2 to make them correct.

$$\boxed{} + \boxed{} - \boxed{} = 7$$

$$\boxed{} + \boxed{} + \boxed{} = 20$$

$$\boxed{} - \boxed{} + \boxed{} = 6$$

$$\boxed{} + \boxed{} - \boxed{} = 2$$

$$\boxed{} + \boxed{} + \boxed{} = 15$$

$$\boxed{} - \boxed{} + \boxed{} = 12$$

Learning objectives

• To use addition and subtraction facts to solve number puzzles

Guidance notes

Your child may need to use trial and error methods to calculate the correct position for each of the numbers, but try to encourage them to become more sophisticated in their choice.

You will need
- A pencil

27 mistakes

Can you find 27 mistakes in this multiplication grid? Put a ring around each wrong answer

×	2	3	4	5	6	7	8	9	10
2	4	6	8	9	11	13	16	18	20
3	6	9	10	15	18	21	23	27	30
4	8	11	16	20	24	28	32	35	40
5	10	14	20	24	30	36	40	44	50
6	12	19	24	30	36	42	48	53	60
7	14	20	28	36	42	48	56	62	70
8	16	25	32	41	49	55	64	71	80
9	18	27	35	45	54	63	71	81	90
10	20	30	40	45	50	60	80	90	100

Learning objectives

- To know multiplication facts up to 10 x 10

Guidance notes

Encourage your child to check each calculation in order to identify the errors.

How big is your name?

To find how big your name is you add up the numbers given to each letter in your name using the table below:

Letter	A	B	C	D	E	F	G	H	I	J	K	L	M
Value	1	2	3	4	5	6	7	8	9	10	11	12	13

Letter	N	O	P	Q	R	S	T	U	V	W	X	Y	Z
Value	14	15	16	17	18	19	20	21	22	23	24	25	26

For example: JOHN   J = 10 O = 15 H = 8 N = 14
So JOHN is   10 + 15 + 8 + 14 = 47

How big are the following names?

1.   MARY

2.   JEAN

3.   ALI

Can you find a name:

4.   Bigger than 70?

5.   Bigger than 80?

What is the biggest name you can find?

Learning objectives

• Solving mathematical problems
• Quick and accurate addition of one- and two-digit numbers

Guidance notes

When your child has finished, check the totals and help with any he or she found difficult.

Number search

How many groups of three numbers can you join so that they make a number sentence?
You can join numbers horizontally, vertically or diagonally.

Example: $12 \times 2 = 24$
             $24 \div 2 = 12$

Can you make 10 addition, subtraction, multiplication and division sentences? There are many more than 10 to be found.

3	4	12	9	3	3
7	5	6	2	8	16
21	20	2	18	24	17
7	4	10	40	8	48
22	48	26	2	16	10
15	12	36	3	8	24
6	45	5	9	2	14
9	15	3	12	4	6

Learning objectives

• To know addition facts and corresponding subtraction facts, and multiplication facts and corresponding division facts
Vocabulary: inverse operation

Guidance notes

Encourage your child to identify and record the inverse operations of each calculation they find, as in the example above.

You will need
- A pencil and paper

Making numbers

Using the digits 2, 3 and 6 and any of the operations $+$, $-$, x, $\div$, how many different numbers can you make in 15 minutes? You must use all three digits each time. Put your numbers in order, starting with the smallest one.

Example: $6 \div 3 + 2 = 4$

Learning objectives

- Addition, subtraction, multiplication and division of whole numbers
- Simple fractions
- Ordering number including negative numbers

Vocabulary: digit, operation, negative

Guidance notes

Encourage your child to include whole numbers, fractions and possibly negative numbers:
e.g. $3/6 + 2 = 2^1/_2$ and $2 + 3 - 6 = -1$

When your child has finished, check the answers and talk about any which are incorrect. A common mistake is to think that -1 is less than -2.

Make 50p

Find all the ways that you can to make 50p exactly.

For example: 20p + 20p + 10p = 50p

or 20p + 20p + 5p + 5p = 50p

Write your answers here:

....

....

....

....

Write the largest number of coins needed to make 50p...

Write the smallest number of coins needed to make 50p...

Learning objectives

• To be able to solve money problems using the appropriate operation, working out which coins to use in a systematic way

Guidance notes

Read through the instructions so that you can help your child understand what has to be done. Encourage him or her to work in a systematic way, by finding all the ways of making 50p with both 20p coins first and varying the other coins. Then all the ways using only one 20p coin and, finally, ways of making the amount without using the 20p coin.

You will need
• A pencil

A difference square

−	66	14	9	53	32	48	20
84	16	70	75	31	52	38	64
8	58	6	1	47	26	40	12
71	5	85	62	18	37	23	51
21	45	7	12	(34)	11	37	1
50	16	36	41	3	28	2	40
14	52	28	5	39	18	34	6
36	30	22	27	27	4	12	16

In the above difference square there are 12 mistakes.

One has already been circled.

Find the remaining 11 mistakes and put a circle around each one.

The square is made up in the following way. The number in the square, for example 34, is obtained by finding the difference between the number in the left-hand column opposite it (21) and the number in the top row directly above it (53). Because the difference between 53 and 21 is 32 and not 34, the number 34 is ringed.

Learning objectives

• Quick and accurate subtraction of pairs of one- and two-digit numbers

Guidance notes

Explain to your child how the difference square is made up: for example, the number in the bottom right-hand corner is obtained by finding the difference between 36 (left-hand column opposite) and 20 (top row, above). When your child has finished, check the ringed numbers with him or her.

You will need
- A blank die with the faces numbered 3–8
- Two sets of counters

Is it the same shape?

A game for two players

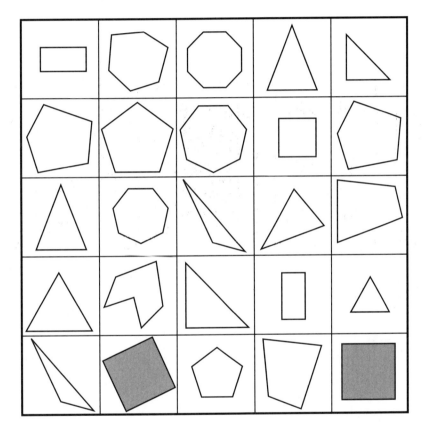

You need a die numbered 3, 4, 5, 6, 7, 8, and different coloured counters for each player. Each person throws a die and covers the shape that has the same number of sides as the number on the die. The player must be able to name the shape before it can be covered. For example: a player throws a three, then has to select which triangle to cover and says, "I will cover the scalene triangle".

If a player recognises any shapes as congruent (identical in size and shape) and identifies them successfully, then all identified shapes may be covered, as in the shaded example of the squares.

The winner is the first person to cover three shapes in a row, in a column or diagonally.

Learning objectives

- To be able to recognise and name 2D shapes by knowing their properties
- To know and use the term 'congruent'

Vocabulary: scalene triangle, congruent

Guidance notes

Read through the instructions with your child. You may need to help him or her find the shape that matches the number on the die. Encourage him or her to say the name of the shape before it is covered.

Name

Class **Date**

You will need
• A pack of playing cards

Adding to 27

A card game for one player

 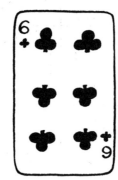   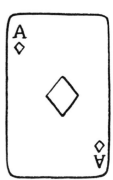

Shuffle the pack of cards.
Turn the cards over one at a time and then place them in a row going from left to right.
When you have a set of cards next to each other that have a total of 27, take them away.
Note – Jack, Queens and Kings each are worth 10.
Continue until you have used all the cards.
Play this game a number of times and try to finish with as few cards in the row as you can.

Learning objectives

• Quick and accurate addition of sets of two or more
  numbers to make a total of 27
Vocabulary: row, total, add

Guidance notes

Explain to your child how to play the game. In the picture above the cards, 6, Jack, 10, Ace add to make 27 so they are taken away and the next card that is turned over is placed to the right of the 7 of hearts.

You will need
• Tape measure or ruler
• A pencil
• Household objects chosen from the list below

Estimating and measuring 1

Choose from the items below those which you would estimate as less than 50mm long.

A sweet, a pin, a paperclip, a pea, a coin, a rubber, an earring, a key, a can
Write the name of the item, your estimate and then the actual measurement.

ITEM .... ESTIMATE .... mm MEASUREMENT .... mm

ITEM .... ESTIMATE .... mm MEASUREMENT .... mm

ITEM .... ESTIMATE .... mm MEASUREMENT .... mm

ITEM .... ESTIMATE .... mm MEASUREMENT .... mm

ITEM .... ESTIMATE .... mm MEASUREMENT .... mm

Choose from the items below those you would estimate as less than 30cm long.

A can, a mug, a vase, a bottle, a fork, a book, a newspaper, an umbrella, a cereal packet.
Record your estimates and actual measurements as before.

ITEM .... ESTIMATE .... cm MEASUREMENT .... cm

ITEM .... ESTIMATE .... cm MEASUREMENT .... cm

ITEM .... ESTIMATE .... cm MEASUREMENT .... cm

ITEM .... ESTIMATE .... cm MEASUREMENT .... cm

ITEM .... ESTIMATE .... cm MEASUREMENT .... cm

Learning objectives

• To estimate and check the height, length or width of objects using millimetres and centimetres

Guidance notes

Read through the instructions with your child. Make sure he or she estimates first and writes the approximate measurement before checking.

You may want to show your child how to place the ruler/tape measure on the object to help him or her measure.

Number chains

Put the number 6 in the start box and follow the arrows in the chain. Every circle contains an instruction (it tells you what to do with your number). You should finish with the number 3 in the answer box.

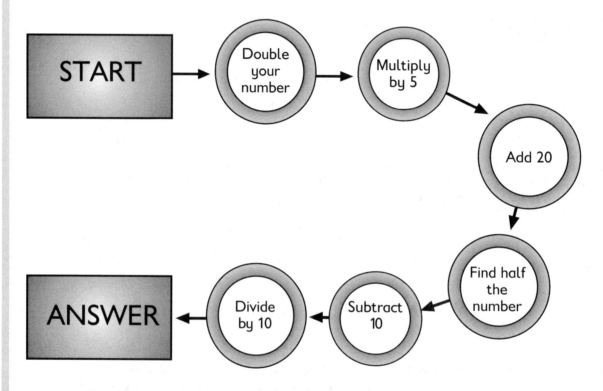

Now try these start numbers:

1. 8 ....

2. 7 ....

3. 9 ....

4. 11 ....

Learning objectives

• Accurately following a series of instructions involving addition, subtraction, multiplication and division of whole numbers and simple fractions

Guidance notes

You may need to show your child how to complete the number chain by working through with the start number 6.

When your child has finished, check the answers and talk about the link between the start numbers and the answers.

You will need
- Counters
- The questions on this sheet

Guess the shape

A game for two players

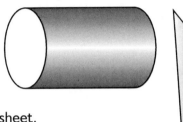

One player chooses one of the 3D shapes on this sheet.
The other player asks the questions below in order, receiving yes or no answers, until he or she has recognised the shape.

For example,
Player 1 (choosing the cube): I'm thinking of a shape.
Player 2: Has it more than 4 faces?
Player 1: Yes.
Player 2 covers the tetrahedron, sphere, cylinder and the cone, which do not have more than 4 faces.
Player 2: Do any faces have right angles?
Player 1: Yes.
Player 2 covers the octahedron as it has no right angles.
Player 2 has to choose between the cube and the cuboid.
Player 2: Are all the faces the same shape?
Player 1: Yes.
Player 2: It's the cube.

Then player 2 chooses a shape and asks the questions.

Questions to ask:

- Has it more than 4 faces?
- Do any faces have any right-angles?
- Are all the faces the same shape?
- Has it a circular face?
- Has it two identical end faces?
- Has it a curved edge?

Learning objectives

- To be able to classify 3D shapes using criteria such as number and shape of faces
Vocabulary: octahedron

Guidance notes

Read through the instructions so that you can help your child understand how to play the game. You may have to help him or her read the questions.

Covering the shapes that do not meet the criteria each time in response to the answers will help your child to look carefully at the properties of those uncovered and choose correctly.

Name

Class   **Date**

You will need
- A pencil and paper for each player
- A die with the numbers from one to six

Make it big

A game for two or more players

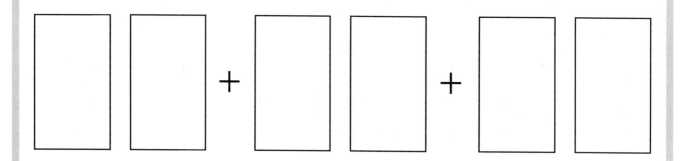

Each player draws the grid, as above, on their paper. Players take it in turns to throw the die. All players put the number thrown in one of the boxes on their grid. The game finishes after the grid has been filled up and the player who makes the largest total wins that game and gets one point.

The game is played six more times and the winner is the player who scores most points.

Learning objectives

- Working out a strategy for the best position to place the numbers
- Quick and accurate addition of two-digit numbers

Guidance notes

It is helpful if you can play this game with your child.

Encourage your child to think about the 'best' place to put a number and, when the game has finished, check the other players' additions.

Name

Class   **Date**

You will need
• Tape measure or ruler
• A pencil
• Household objects chosen from the list below

Estimating and measuring 2

Choose from the items below that you estimate are over 50cm:

Write the name of the item and estimate in the chart below. Then measure and record in the chart.

ITEM .... ESTIMATE .... cm MEASUREMENT .... cm

ITEM .... ESTIMATE .... cm MEASUREMENT .... cm

ITEM .... ESTIMATE .... cm MEASUREMENT .... cm

ITEM .... ESTIMATE .... cm MEASUREMENT .... cm

Choose from the items listed below those that you estimate are over 1 metre:
chair, bed, clothes line, gate, windowsill, coat, door, waste bin and drawer

Record in the chart, as before.

ITEM .... ESTIMATE .... m MEASUREMENT .... m

ITEM .... ESTIMATE .... m MEASUREMENT .... m

ITEM .... ESTIMATE .... m MEASUREMENT .... m

ITEM .... ESTIMATE .... m MEASUREMENT .... m

Learning objectives

• To estimate and measure objects using centimetres and metres

Guidance notes

Read through the instructions with your child. Make sure he or she estimates first and writes the approximate measurement before checking.

You may want to show your child how to place the ruler/tape measure on the object to help him or her measure.

Name

Class   **Date**

You will need
• A pencil and paper

Dart to 50

In 15 minutes, how many different ways can you find to score 50 by throwing 3 darts? You are only allowed to score using the numbers 1 to 20, the 25 ring and bull's eye (50). Make a list of your answers.

Learning objectives

• Quick and accurate addition of 3 numbers totalling 50
• Reasoning to find a systematic way of finding different combinations

Guidance notes

Explain to your child that he or she cannot use the doubles or trebles on the dart board.

When your child has finished, check his or her answers.

You will need
Squared paper
Ruler

Shape up

If you plot the co-ordinates below on to a grid and join the points in order using a ruler you will make a square.

(1,1) (1,5) (5,5) (5,1) (1,1)

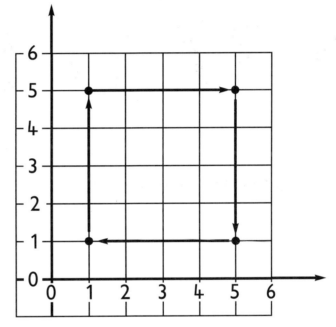

Can you guess what shapes these co-ordinates will make?
Draw out an 8×8 grid on squared paper for each set of co-ordinates and see if you guessed correctly.
Remember to join up the co-ordinates in order, use straight lines. Can you name all the shapes?

1.   (1,1) (2,5) (6,5) (5,1) (1,1)

2.   (0,0) (4,1) (4,5) (0,4) (0,0)

3.   (6,3) (1,5) (4,0) (4,6) (1,1) (6,3)

4.   (4,4) (6,2) (4,0) (2,2) (4.4)

5.   (5,8) (8,6) (5,1) (2,6) (5,8)

6.   (2,6) (4,6) (5,3) (4,0) (2,0) (1,3) (2,6)

7.   (3,1) (1,3) (1,5) (3,7) (5,7) (7,5) (7,3) (5,1) (3,1)

8.   (1,1) (4,5) (5,1) (1,1)

Learning objectives

- To read and plot co-ordinates in the first quadrant
- To name 2D shapes

Guidance notes

Your child may need help in plotting the co-ordinates. Make sure they go along first and then up.

You will need
• A pencil

Take two

Choose two numbers each time from

21 37 41 53 66

to make each of the following number sentences.

1. .... + ... = 90

2. .... − .... = 29

3. .... + ... = 94

4. .... + 16 = ...

5. .... − 25 = ...

6. .... − 29 = ...

Learning objectives

• Addition and subtraction of two two-digit numbers
• Finding a strategy
Vocabulary: number sentences

Guidance notes

Encourage your child to find a strategy for finding the correct numbers.

When your child has finished, check the answers and help with any he or she found difficult.

You will need
• A calculator may be useful

Two missing numbers

I am thinking of two numbers.
If I add the numbers the total is 14.
If I subtract the numbers the difference is 4.
If I multiply the two numbers the product is 45.
Which two numbers am I thinking of?

Can you find the two missing numbers for these puzzles?

The total is 13.
The difference is 1.
The product is 42.
What are the two numbers? ___ ___

Total = 15.
Difference = 9.
Product = 36.
What are the two numbers? ___ ___

Total = 27.
Difference = 13.
Product = 140.
What are the two numbers? ___ ___

Total = 27.
Difference = 7.
Product = 170.
What are the two numbers? ___ ___

Total = 26.
Difference = 4.
Product = 165.
What are the two numbers? ___ ___

Total = 48.
Difference = 2.
Product = 575.
What are the two numbers? ___ ___

Learning objectives	Guidance notes
• To solve number puzzles **Vocabulary**: total, difference, product	Encourage your child to try different methods for finding the answers.

Making 88

| 1 | 2 | 3 | 4 | 5 | 6 | 7 | 8 |

Using all of the cards above once and only once and in any order with any number of addition and subtraction signs, how close can you get to making 88?

For example: $18 + 27 + 56 - 3 - 4 = 94$

If you are successful in making 88, can you find more than one way of making it? Write your answers down.

Learning objectives

- Quick addition and subtraction of a number of one- and two-digit numbers
- Thinking quickly and logically to discard any combinations that cannot make 88

Guidance notes

Your child will need to cut out a number of small cards and write on them the numbers 1–8 and a few addition and subtraction signs.

When your child has tried this puzzle for 15 minutes, talk to him or her about the answers.

Number puzzles

1. Subtract 5.
The answer is 24.
What is the number?

2. Divide by 3.
The answer is 25.
What is the number?

3. Multiply by 10.
The answer is 80.
What is the number?

4. Divide by 10, subtract 2.
The answer is 8.
What is the number?

5. Add 25, divide by 2.
The answer is 40.
What is the number?

6. Double the number,
add 4, multiply by 5.
The answer is 40.
What is the number?

Now make up some number puzzles of your own to test out on someone else!

Learning objectives

• To solve number puzzles
Vocabulary: inverse operations

Guidance notes

Your child will need to work out what the inverse operation is each time in order to calculate the answers.

You will need
• A pencil and paper

Cross number puzzle

	Across		Down
1	112×3	1	386 to the nearest 10
3	$83 - 49$	2	How many tens in 360?
5	$27 + 32 + 37$	3	$660 \div 2 = \ldots\ldots$
6	$\ldots\ldots - 42 = 193$	4	$^3/_{10}$ of 150
7	$56 + 54$	6	$2000 - 1784$
8	253×2	7	One quarter of 408
10	Double 51	8	471 to the nearest 100
11	Divide 200 by 4	9	$34 + 36 + 37$
12	4 squared add 4	10	$^1/_{10}$ of 120
13	The next number in the sequence 79, 86, 93, 100	11	$^1/_4$ of 200

Learning objectives

• Solving number problems using the four rules
• Rounding numbers and use of fractions

Guidance notes

Explain to your child that the answers should be written on the puzzle.

Check the answers when finished and talk about any that were difficult.

Name

Class   **Date**

You will need
• A calculator

Consecutive numbers

When I multiply two consecutive numbers together I get an answer of 56.
Which two numbers did I multiply? ____ ____

Now try these.
Which two consecutive numbers have a product of:

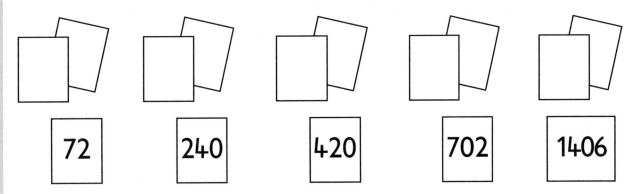

| 72 | 240 | 420 | 702 | 1406 |

Which three consecutive numbers would I need to multiply to get these answers?

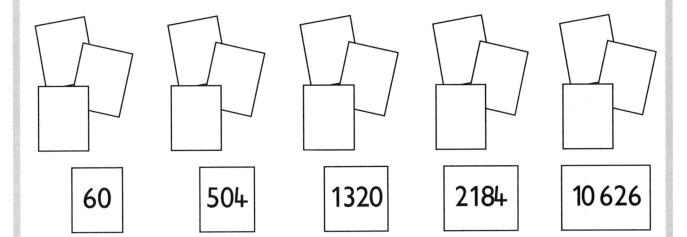

| 60 | 504 | 1320 | 2184 | 10 626 |

Learning objectives

• To find two consecutive numbers with a given product
• To find three consecutive numbers with a given product

Guidance notes

Your child may need to trial several numbers and adjust their answers when they have worked out the product before they find the correct numbers.

Hitting the target

Using any three numbers from the list of four below, complete the number sentences to make the target numbers on the right-hand side of each number sentence.

12 14 17 19

1.   .... + ... + ... = 50

2.   .... + ... + ... = 45

3.   .... + ... − .... = 16

4.   .... + ... − .... = 7

5.   .... − .... + ... = 21

6.   .... + ... − .... = 24

Learning objectives

• Addition and subtraction of three two-digit numbers
• Finding a strategy for choice of numbers and quick addition and subtraction

Vocabulary: number sentences

Guidance notes

Encourage your child to try and find a strategy for finding the correct numbers and adding or subtracting them quickly.

When your child has finished, talk about any he or she found difficult.

Name

Class   **Date**

You will need
• 1p, 2p, 5p, 10p, 20p, 50p coins

Smallest amount of coins

Using the least number of coins each time fill in the grid to show how many are needed to make all the amounts up to 50p. The first row is completed for you.

1p	2p	3p	4p	5p	6p	7p	8p	9p	10p
1 *coin*	*1* *coin*	*2* *coins*	*2* *coins*	*1* *coin*	*2* *coins*	*2* *coins*	*3* *coins*	*3* *coins*	*1* *coin*
11p	12p	13p	14p	15p	16p	17p	18p	19p	20p
21p	22p	23p	24p	25p	26p	27p	28p	29p	30p
31p	32p	33p	34p	35p	36p	37p	38p	39p	40p
41p	42p	43p	44p	45p	46p	47p	48p	49p	50p

Which amounts of money require the most coins?

Write the amounts here ....

Predict which amounts of money up to £1 would take at least six coins to make them exactly.

Write the amounts here ....

Learning objectives

• To be able to solve problems using money

Guidance notes

Read through the instructions with your child.

It is important to emphasise that the fewest coins are to be chosen each time.

You will need
• A pencil and paper

Mind the gap

In the problems below put a single digit in each hole to make each calculation correct.

$$
\begin{array}{r}
25 \\
+\ 3\square \\
\hline
61
\end{array}
\qquad
\begin{array}{r}
2\square \\
-\ 18 \\
\hline
11
\end{array}
\qquad
\begin{array}{r}
2\square \\
+\ \square 0 \\
\hline
58
\end{array}
$$

$$
\begin{array}{r}
3\square \\
+\ \square 7 \\
\hline
111
\end{array}
\qquad
\begin{array}{r}
\square 6 \\
+\ 6\square \\
\hline
81
\end{array}
\qquad
\begin{array}{r}
100 \\
-\ \square\square \\
\hline
67
\end{array}
$$

$$
\begin{array}{r}
123 \\
-\ 3\square \\
\hline
\square 1
\end{array}
\qquad
\begin{array}{r}
103 \\
-\ \square 4 \\
\hline
5\square
\end{array}
$$

Learning objectives

• Reasoning and solving problems involving addition and subtraction of two- and three-digit numbers

Guidance notes

You may need to explain to your child that in each box you can only place a single digit (from 0 to 9 inclusive).

Encourage your child to start with the units digit first.

You will need
- A pencil
- A right-angled marker
- A can
- A mug or glass
- A packet
- A video tape

Perpendicular

Collect together a can, a packet, a video tape and a straight-sided mug or glass.

Place them on the table in an upright position. All these objects are perpendicular to the table. You can check this by making a right-angled marker and placing the marker next to each object as is shown in the pictures below.

Look around inside and outside your home to find other objects that are perpendicular. Write your list here, or draw your objects on the back of this sheet.

Two to start you off are:
A rotary clothes line
A door

Learning objectives

- To know that perpendicular lines are at right angles to each other
- To be able to recognise them in the environment

Vocabulary: perpendicular

Guidance notes

Read through the instructions so that you can help your child understand what has to be done. Allow him or her to complete each part before reading the next instruction.

You may have to help your child to make the right-angled marker from a scrap of paper, and walk around your home identifying objects that are perpendicular.

An addition square

+	16	22	31	45	38	19	9	44
25	41	47	56	70	63	54	34	69
14	30	46	45	59	62	33	23	58
33	49	55	64	(68)	71	52	44	77
46	62	68	67	91	84	65	55	90
9	25	31	40	54	49	28	18	53
40	56	72	71	85	78	59	49	84
37	33	59	68	82	75	66	46	71
23	39	45	53	68	61	41	32	67

In the above addition square there are 13 mistakes.

One has already been circled.

Find the remaining 12 mistakes and put a circle around each one.

Learning objectives

- Quick and accurate addition of pairs of one- and two-digit numbers

Guidance notes

Explain to your child how the addition square is made up: for example, the number 68, which is ringed, is obtained by adding the number in the left-hand column opposite it (33) to the number in the top row directly above it (45). Because 33 + 45 = 78, the number 68 is ringed. When your child has finished, check the ringed numbers with him or her.

Name

Class   **Date**

Parallel

Collect together rectangular or square objects such as a packet, a box, a placemat or a book. Place them on the table.

All of these objects have parallel lines.

You can check this by measuring across them with a tape measure or ruler. The opposite edges should be the same distance apart.

Look around inside and outside your home to find other objects that are parallel. Write them here:

Outside
A fence

Inside
A book
A staircase

A mathematical word search

1. How many pairs of gloves can you make from 39 gloves? ....

2. What number multiplied by itself makes 16? ....

3. How many pence change do I get from £1 if I buy 2 biros costing 27p each? ....

4. One third of 90 is ....

5. How many hours in three-quarters of a day? ....

6. How many months are there in 6 years? ....

7. What is the next number 30, 37, 44, ...?

8. The sum of 16, 25, 26 is ....

9. What is two-thirds of 30? ....

10. The difference between 220 and 127 is ....

11. How many kilometres is 5000 metres? ....

N	I	N	E	T	Y	T	H	R	E	E	Z	J	N
F	O	U	R	S	D	G	S	M	G	T	P	N	I
Y	K	T	H	D	L	T	Q	P	O	H	A	E	N
F	O	R	T	Y	S	I	X	F	L	I	Q	D	E
X	Y	Q	T	W	E	N	T	Y	L	R	S	Z	T
E	H	S	P	L	V	T	J	P	O	T	A	E	E
I	K	T	H	D	E	K	Q	S	T	Y	A	L	E
G	A	P	H	S	N	G	R	P	O	X	A	K	N
H	O	K	H	D	T	T	W	K	S	L	F	Y	O
T	F	I	F	T	Y	O	N	E	K	D	I	T	G
E	R	T	H	D	T	G	P	D	N	S	V	W	S
E	J	S	H	D	W	T	A	P	R	I	E	R	K
N	K	T	H	D	O	Z	Q	K	G	O	A	S	Q
Y	S	I	X	T	Y	S	E	V	E	N	A	L	T

Find the answers to each of the questions above. The answers are written in words either horizontally or vertically in the word search. When you have found the word put a ring around it.

Learning objectives

• Addition, subtraction, multiplication and division of whole numbers
• Simple fractions
• Solving problems involving money, time and length

Guidance notes

Explain to your child what has to be done, if he or she is unsure.

When your child has finished, talk about the answers and link them to the words in the word search.

Name

Class　　**Date**

Find the areas

Collect together these small rectangular objects.

Measure the length and the width of the audio cassette holder first. Round the measurement to the nearest centimetre.

Length .... cm

Width .... cm

To find the area of the shape, multiply the length by the width.
As a formula this can be written as lxw (length x width)
The area of the cassette holder is .... cm².

You can check this by placing the cassette holder on centimetre squared paper.

Now work out how the areas of the other objects you have chosen.
Remember to measure the length and width first.

The area of the CD holder is .... cm²

The area of the postage stamp is .... cm²

The area of the video cassette is .... cm²

Explain how you worked out your answers

....

....

Name	
Class	Date

You will need
- A pencil and paper

Number chains

Put the number 5 in the start box and follow the arrows in the chain. Every circle contains an instruction (it tells you what to do with your number). You should finish with the number 7 in the answer box.

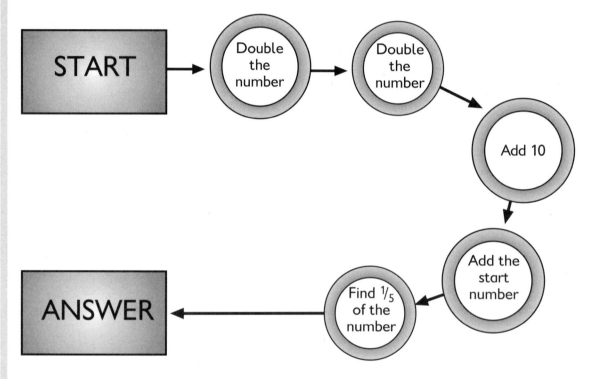

Now try these start numbers:

1.   6 ....

2.   9 ....

3.   11 ....

4.   1½ ....

Learning objectives

- Accurately following a series of instructions involving addition, doubling, division and fractions.

Guidance notes

You may need to show your child how to complete the number chain by working through with the start number 5.

When your child has finished, check the answers and talk about the link between the start numbers and the answers.

You will need
• A pencil

Fill the gaps

Find the missing numbers in these addition and multiplication grids.

+	14	29
11	25	
13		

×	6	7
9		
8		

+	15	9	27	32
19				
27				
34				
45				

×	9	8	6	7
5				
7				
9				
6				

Learning objectives

• To develop quick recall of addition and multiplication facts

Guidance notes

You may need to check that your child knows how to complete each grid before he or she starts.

Name

Class　　　　**Date**

Making 100

A game for two or more players

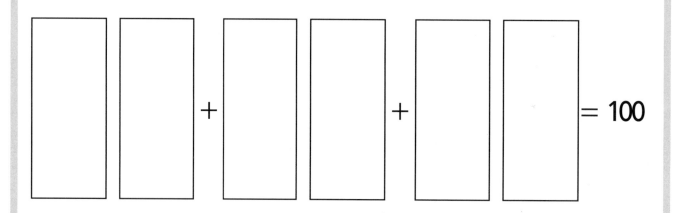

Each player draws the grid, as above, on their paper. Players take it in turns to throw the die. All players put the number thrown in one of the boxes on their grid. The game finishes after the grid has been filled up and the player who makes a total nearest to 100 (above or below) gets one point.

The game is played six more times and the winner is the player who scores most points.

Learning objectives

- Working out a strategy for the best position to place the numbers
- Quick and accurate addition of two-digit numbers

Guidance notes

It is helpful if you can play this game with your child.

Encourage your child to check the other players' additions to ensure they are correct.

Fraction triangles

Can you see how the fractions on this triangle have been worked out?

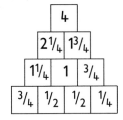

You add the two fractions in the squares directly below. For example:

$3/4 + 1/2 = 11/4$

Work out the missing numbers in these fraction triangles.

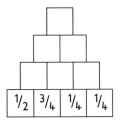

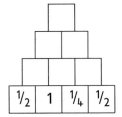

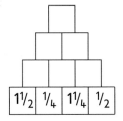

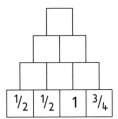

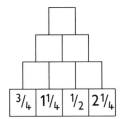

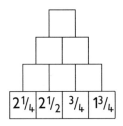

Make up some more triangles of your own on another piece of paper.

Learning objectives

• To add fractions, including whole numbers, halves and quarters

Guidance notes

You may need to check that your child knows how to complete each triangle.

You will need
- A pencil and paper

Making numbers
3 6 12

Using the numbers 3, 6 and 12 and any of the operations +, −, ×, ÷, how many different numbers can you make in 15 minutes? You must use all three numbers each time. Put your numbers in order starting with the smallest one. You can have fractions and negative numbers. Write your answers here:

Learning objectives

- Addition, subtraction, multiplication and division of one- and two-digit numbers
- Simple fractions
- Ordering numbers, including negative numbers and fractions

Vocabulary: operation, negative

Guidance notes

Encourage your child to try and include with their list fractions and negative numbers.

For example: $^3/_6 + 12 = 12^1/_2$ and $3 + 6 - 12 = -3$

When your child has finished, check the answers and talk about any that are incorrect. A common mistake is to think that −3 is less than −6.

Symmetry

Find a square piece of paper.

Fold it carefully in half and draw a pattern along the folded edge.

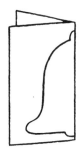

Cut out your design and unfold.

The shape has ONE line of symmetry.

Start with another square of paper. Can you fold it and design and cut out a shape that has TWO lines of symmetry?

Start with a new square of paper each time and see if you can make shapes that have 3 lines of symmetry, 4 lines of symmetry, 5 lines of symmetry!

Learning objectives	Guidance notes
• To recognise lines of symmetry	You may need to help your child fold the paper accurately.

Name

Class   Date

You will need
- Pencil and paper
- A pair of scissors

Making 99

| 1 | 2 | 3 | 4 | 5 | 6 | 7 | 8 | 9 |

Using each of the cards above once and only once, and in any order with any number of addition and subtraction signs, how close can you get to making 99?

For example: $37 + 49 + 28 - 1 - 5 - 6 = 102$

If you are successful in making 99, can you find more than one way of making it? Write your answers down.

Learning objectives

- Quick addition and subtraction of a number of one- and two-digit numbers
- Thinking quickly and logically to discard any combinations that cannot make 99

Guidance notes

Your child will need to cut out a number of small cards and write on them the numbers 1–9 and a few addition and subtraction signs.

When your child has tried this puzzle for 15 minutes, talk to him or her about the answers.

Name

Class **Date**

You will need
- Pencil, ruler or tape measure
- Rectangular objects, such as those shown below

Measure to the nearest millimetre

Collect together four or five rectangular objects.

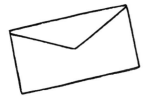  

Write the formula for the perimeter of a rectangle in words.

To find the perimeter of a rectangle ....

....

If you can write the formula in letters and numbers only, write it here: ....

....

Now work out the perimeters of the objects you have chosen.
Remember to measure in millimetres first.

The perimeter of the first object is ....mm.

The perimeter of the second object is ....mm.

The perimeter of the third object is ....mm.

The perimeter of the fourth object is ....mm.

The perimeter of the fifth object is ....mm.

Bingo

A game for two players

Card for First player	4		9	25	16	42	72	24	63	50
	12	81	40	49	80	56	54	48		70

Card for Second player	100	6	35	10	24	36	32	54		20
	90	12	56		45	15	64	50	72	60

Each player takes a card from the pile of cards to decide who starts. The highest card starts.

Each player takes it in turn to take two cards from the top of the pile and multiplies the two numbers together. They then cover that total (if possible) on their card with a counter. The winner is the first person to cover all the numbers on their card.

Learning objectives

- Quick and accurate recall of the 2 to 10 times tables

Guidance notes

It is important to play the game with your child.

When each player has taken two cards, they are put to one side, and when the pile of cards has been used they are shuffled well and the game continues.

Name

Class   **Date**

You will need
• A pencil

Travelling times

The drawing below shows a selection of journeys that a family makes from their home during one week.

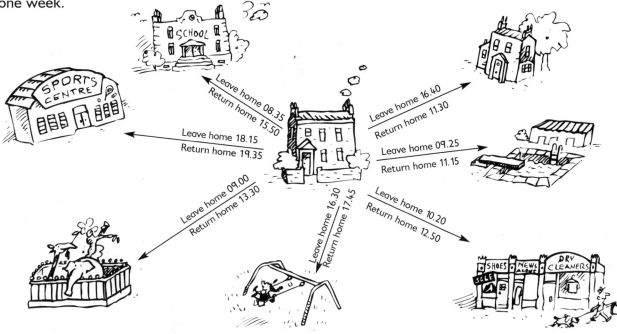

Leave home 08.35
Return home 15.50

Leave home 16.40
Return home 11.30

Leave home 18.15
Return home 19.35

Leave home 09.25
Return home 11.15

Leave home 09.00
Return home 13.30

Leave home 16.30
Return home 17.45

Leave home 10.20
Return home 12.50

Complete the grid with the leaving times and return times for each journey and then work out how long they were away from home on each occasion.

From home to...	Leaving time	Return time	Time away from home
Zoo			
Park			
Sports centre			
School			
Visiting friends			
Swimming pool			
Shops			

Learning objectives

• To read the time and use 24-hour clock notation
• To calculate units of time

Guidance notes

You may need to help your child calculate the difference between the leaving and returning times – particularly to the friend's house, which is an overnight stay!

Hitting the target

Using any three numbers from the list of five below, complete the number sentences to make the target numbers on the right-hand side of each number sentence.

17 23 28 32 41

1. .... + ... + ... = 68

2. .... + ... + ... = 101

3. .... + ... + ... = 72

4. .... + ... + ... = 77

5. .... + ... + ... = 83

6. .... + ... + ... = 96

Number routes

Start at the centre of the grid below. You can move horizontally and vertically around the grid but not diagonally. You have to visit ten squares each time and add up your total. Draw your route each time on the grid and record your totals in the box below.
Do this at least ten times.

82	31	198	76	53	32	40	73	12
177	68	35	90	134	61	13	24	162
56	71	21	73	134	42	85	39	26
31	148	70	27	59	35	75	116	13
128	87	94	56	START	45	89	34	57
167	88	156	23	134	21	87	97	95
48	48	93	24	12	65	93	74	81
34	75	48	63	70	35	23	146	43
186	99	36	86	54	38	77	82	53

What totals did you make?

What was the biggest total you made? ....
What was the smallest total? ....

Learning objectives

• To add strings of two- and three-digit numbers
• To check the sum of several numbers by adding in the reverse order

Guidance notes

Encourage your child to find different routes looking for the smallest total possible and the largest total possible, and to check their answers by adding the same numbers in reverse order.

4, 4, 4, 4

Using all four 4s above, how many different whole numbers can you make in 15 minutes? You must use all four 4s each time. You can use any operation of +, −, x, ÷. You are also allowed to write the digits together to make 44. Put all your answers in order.

An example to help you: 24 = 4 x 4 + 4 + 4
Write your answers here:

Name	
Class	Date

You will need
- A pencil
- A ruler or tape measure
- Millimetre squared paper
- Rectangular objects such as those shown below
- A calculator

Finding smaller areas

Collect together these small rectangular objects.

Measure the length and width of the playing card first

Length ....mm.
Width ....mm.

Write the formula to calculate the area of a rectangle in words: To find the area of a
rectangle ....

The area of the playing card is ....mm².

You can check this by placing the playing card on millimetre squared paper.

Now work out the areas of the other objects you have chosen.
Remember to measure the length and width first.

The area of the postage stamp is ....mm².

The area of the birthday card is ....mm².

The area of the postcard is ....mm².

The area of the ruler is ....mm².

Learning objectives

- To be able to measure and calculate the area of rectangles
- To be able to explain how to calculate the area of a rectangle using the formula

Vocabulary: square millimetre, mm², formula

Guidance notes

Read through the instructions with your child. You may have to give him or her some help using the formula to work out the answers.

It is important to check the answers with your child to make sure the measuring is accurate and that he or she understands how to calculate the area.

Name

Class   **Date**

You will need
- A pencil

Number sequences in a square

124	118	112	106	100						↴
1·2	1·4	1·6	1·8	2·0					↴	
11	22	33	44	55				↴		
96	91	86	81				↴			
100	110	120	130			↴				
3	7	11	15		↴					
6	12	18	24	↴						
3	6	9	12↴							
2	4	6↴								
■	8									
■	10									

Complete the sequences by going along each row and down the column following the arrow.
The first one has been done for you.

Learning objectives

- Finding a pattern in a series of numbers and counting backwards and forwards in different amounts from varied starting points
- Numbers including decimals

Guidance notes

When your child has completed the pattern, talk about the answers and the patterns found and help with any found difficult.

Name

Class **Date**

You will need
• Household items, such as those shown below

Measuring in tenths of a litre

You will need a litre jug or half-litre jug that is marked in 100ml units, and some empty household containers.

Estimate how much each container holds to the nearest 100ml and fill in the sentences below. Then check by pouring from the household container to the litre jug.

Write your answers in ml, or decimal fractions of a litre: for example, 500ml or 0·5l.

I estimate the .... holds .... ml. I measured and found that the .... holds .... ml, or .... litre.

I estimate the .... holds .... ml. I measured and found that the .... holds .... ml, or .... litre.

I estimate the .... holds .... ml. I measured and found that the .... holds .... ml, or .... litre.

I estimate the .... holds .... ml. I measured and found that the .... holds .... ml, or .... litre.

I estimate the .... holds .... ml. I measured and found that the .... holds .... ml, or .... litre.

Learning objectives

• To record estimates and measurements in ml, and tenths of a litre. For example, that 700ml is 0.7l
• To read a simple scale to the nearest tenth of a litre

Guidance notes

It would be helpful if your child could collect the items for one question and do this activity practically before writing the answer and moving on to the next question.

You will probably need to help your child pour from one container to the next, especially if the container chosen is more than a litre.

Remember to ask your child to estimate first.

Darting doubles

In 15 minutes, how many different ways can you find to score 62 by throwing 3 darts? You must include at least one double (but no trebles), and can, of course, use the 25 and bull's eye (50). Make a list of your answers.

Learning objectives

• Quick and accurate doubling of numbers and addition of three numbers totalling 62
• Reasoning to find a systematic way of finding different combinations

Guidance notes

Explain to your child, if necessary, how you can score doubles and what trebles mean. When your child has finished, check the answers.

Odds and evens

Continue this pattern: 2, 4, 6, 8, ..., ..., ..., ...
These are EVEN numbers.

Continue this pattern: 1, 3, 5, 7, ..., ..., ..., ...
These are ODD numbers.

Add these EVEN numbers together:

$4 + 8 =$ ....
$12 + 4 =$ ....
$28 + 36 =$ ....
$126 + 58 =$ ....
$244 + 76 =$ ....

What do you notice about all the answers?

Add these ODD numbers together:

$1 + 7 =$ ....
$35 + 17 =$ ....
$49 + 21 =$ ....
$131 + 61 =$ ....
$243 + 63 =$ ....

What do you notice about these answers?

What happens when you add an even number to an odd number or vice versa?
Try out several sums to find out.

Complete the grid below.

+	EVEN	ODD
EVEN		
ODD		

Find out what happens when you multiply odd and even numbers.

×	EVEN	ODD
EVEN		
ODD		

Learning objectives

• To make general statements about odd and even numbers

Guidance notes

Your child will need to work out each calculation and then complete each grid.

A number puzzle

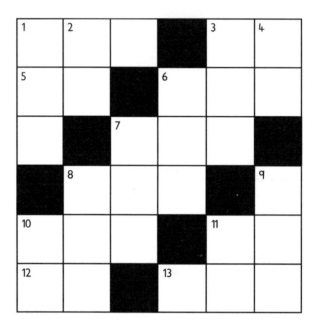

	Across		Down
1	50% of £300 = £..........	1	Round 148.2 to the nearest whole number
3	Double 8½	2	One quarter of 200
5	£39.80 rounded to the nearest pound =	3	Twice 85
6	What number is halfway between 650 and 700?	4	425 + ... = 500
7	How many £10 notes in £1300?	6	633 rounded to the nearest 10
8	How many times larger is 2500 than 25?	7	.... + 62 = 170
10	.... + 626 = 884	8	25% of 600
11	¼ of 48	9	4×30
12	Decrease 132 by 42	10	806 − 777
13	80×6	11	¾ of 24

Learning objectives

• Solving number problems using the four rules
• Rounding numbers
• Fractions, decimals and percentages

Guidance notes

Explain to your child the answers should be written in figures on the puzzle.

Check the answers when finished and talk about any difficult ones.

Name

Class		Date	

You will need
- A pencil

School timetable

ACTIVITY	START TIME	DIGITAL TIME	24-HOUR TIME
START SCHOOL	Five to nine in the morning		
ASSEMBLY	Quarter past nine in the morning		
LITERACY HOUR	Twenty-five to ten in the morning		
BREAKTIME	Twenty to eleven in the morning		
NUMERACY HOUR	Eleven o'clock in the morning		
LUNCHTIME	Ten past twelve		
START OF AFTERNOON	Twenty past one in the afternoon		
END OF SCHOOL TIME	A quarter to four in the afternoon		
AFTER-SCHOOL CLUB	Four o'clock in the afternoon		
SCHOOL MEETING FOR PARENTS	Half past seven in the evening		

This is an example of a timetable: fill in the gaps. Ask an adult to check your answers before you answer the following questions.

1.   How long does assembly last? ....

2.   How long is the lunchtime? ....

3.   How long is the afternoon session? ....

4.   If after-school clubs last three-quarters of an hour, at what time do they finish?

   ....

5.   If the evening meeting for parents is one hour and fifty minutes, what time does the meeting finish? ....

Learning objectives

- To be able to know the a.m. and p.m. equivalents in 24-hour time
- To be able to read timetables

Guidance notes

Read through the instructions with your child.

You may need to help your child to read the time in words, then encourage him or her to say the time digitally before writing it.

Name

Class   **Date**

You will need
• A pencil and paper

Mind the gap

In the problems below, put a single digit in each hole to make each calculation correct.

$$
\begin{array}{r}
37 \\
+\ 4\ \square \\
\hline
82
\end{array}
\qquad
\begin{array}{r}
3\ \square \\
-\ 14 \\
\hline
19
\end{array}
\qquad
\begin{array}{r}
4\ \square \\
+\ \square\ 1 \\
\hline
78
\end{array}
$$

$$
\begin{array}{r}
6\ \square \\
+\ \square\ 7 \\
\hline
104
\end{array}
\qquad
\begin{array}{r}
\square\ 5 \\
+\ 5\ \square \\
\hline
83
\end{array}
\qquad
\begin{array}{r}
\square\ 00 \\
-\ \square\ \square \\
\hline
24
\end{array}
$$

$$
\begin{array}{r}
109 \\
-\ 4\ \square \\
\hline
\square\ 8
\end{array}
\qquad
\begin{array}{r}
111 \\
-\ \square\ 6 \\
\hline
7\ \square
\end{array}
$$

Learning objectives

• Reasoning and solving problems involving addition and subtraction of two- and three-digit numbers

Guidance notes

You may need to explain to your child that in each box you can only place a single digit (from 0 to 9 inclusive).

Encourage your child to start with the units digit first.

Name	
Class	Date

You will need
- Household items: book, piece of fruit, a vegetable, glass bowl or dish, shoe, opened packet of cereal

Measuring in tenths of a kilogram

You will need a set of scales marked in 100g units, and some household objects to weigh.

Estimate how much your object weighs to the nearest 100g and fill in the sentences below. Then check by weighing the object on the scales.

I estimate the .... holds .... g. I measured and found it
weighs .... g or .... kg

I estimate the .... holds .... g. I measured and found it
weighs .... g or .... kg

I estimate the .... holds .... g. I measured and found it
weighs .... g or .... kg

I estimate the .... holds .... g. I measured and found it
weighs .... g or .... kg

I estimate the .... holds .... g. I measured and found it
weighs .... g or .... kg

Learning objectives
- To record estimates and measurements in tenths of a kilogram: for example, 200g is also 0·2kg
- To read a simple scale to the nearest tenth of a kilogram

Guidance notes
It would be helpful if your child could collect the items for one question and do this activity practically before writing the answer and moving on to the next question.

You will probably need to help your child read the scale to the nearest 100g. Remember to ask your child to estimate first.

You will need
• A pencil

Decimal sums

2·6	2·7	1·6	6·2	9·4	5·1
5·7	4·0	3·4	2·2	6·6	3·3
2·2	0·8	3·0	5·2	7·1	7·2
6·6	1·8	9·0	3·9	8·0	0·6
1·6	8·4	3·0	1·5	4·5	4·0
0·5	7·9	7·0	1·4	0·9	3·1

Can you find two numbers next to each other that add to make 8.4? Draw a ring around them; one has been done for you. Find some more sets of two numbers that add to make 8.4 and draw rings around each of these: there are six sets in total. The pairs of numbers may be horizontal, vertical or diagonal.

Learning objectives

• Quick and accurate addition of pairs of decimal numbers
• Finding a strategy for discarding pairs that obviously cannot make the required sum

Guidance notes

Encourage your child to set a challenge of finding the numbers as quickly as possible.

When your child has finished, check the ringed pairs of numbers and show him or her any he or she may have missed.

Daily temperatures

The January minimum temperatures for different places around the world are shown on the thermometer below. Write the temperatures in the boxes.

Record the July minimum temperatures for the same places on the second thermometer.

- Athens (Greece) 23°C
- Washington (USA) 21°C
- Cape Town (SA) 7°C
- Christchurch (NZ) 1°C
- London (UK) 13°C
- Moscow (Russia) 12°C
- Hong Kong (China) 26°C
- Darwin (Australia) 19°C

Find today's temperatures for these places in today's newspaper. Record them on the third thermometer.

1. If the lowest temperature recorded one day in Cape Town was 15°C and the highest was 26°C, what was the temperature range?_____

2. If the lowest temperature recorded one day in Washington was –1°C and the highest was 7°C, what was the temperature range? _____

3. If the lowest temperature recorded one day in Moscow was –14°C and the highest was –6°C, what was the temperature range?_____

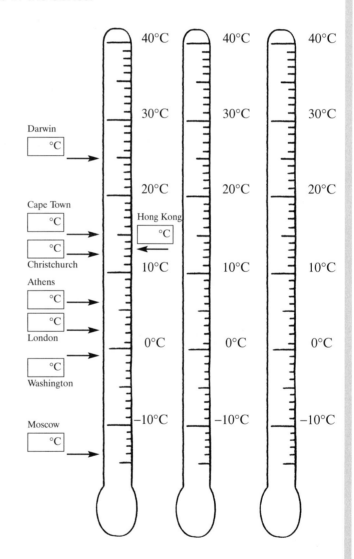

Making numbers

5   10   20

Using the numbers 5, 10 and 20 and any of the operations +, −, ×, ÷, how many different numbers can you make in 20 minutes? You must use all three numbers each time. Put your numbers in order starting with the smallest one. You can have fractions and negative numbers. Write your answers here:

Learning objectives

• Addition, subtraction, multiplication and division of one- and two-digit numbers
• Simple fractions
• Ordering numbers including negatives numbers and fractions

Vocabulary: operation, negative

Guidance notes

Encourage your child to try and include with their list fractions and negative numbers.

For example: $^5/_{20} + 10 = 10^1/_4$ and $5 + 10 − 20 = −5$

When your child has finished, check the answers and talk about any that are incorrect. A common mistake is to think that −4 is less than −5.

Tree diagram

Sort the numbers 1–25 into the tree diagram and write the numbers in the correct boxes.

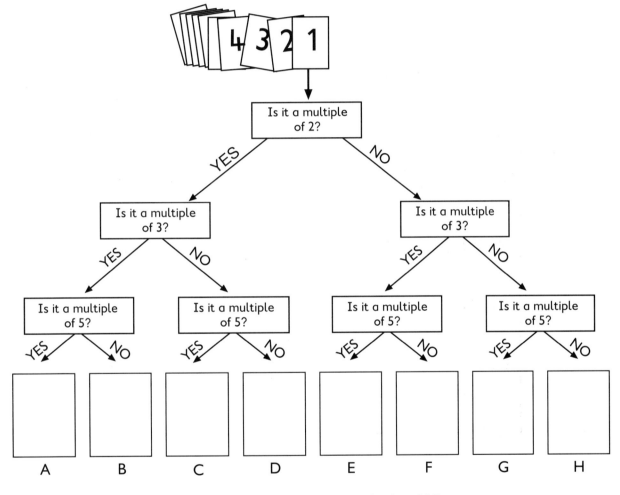

1. Which number is a multiple of 3 and 5 but not a multiple of 2? ....

2. Which numbers are multiples of 5 but not of 2 or 3? ....

3. Which boxes would these numbers go into?

   40 ....   45 ....   30 ....   55 ....

A decimal addition square

+	4·4	7·8	6·3	0·4	1·6	2·9
1·6	6·0	9·6	7·9	2·0	3·2	4·5
0·8	5·2	8·6	7·1	1·2	2·4	10·9
3·7	8·1	11·5	(11·0)	4·1	5·3	6·6
5·2	9·6	14·0	11·5	5·6	6·8	8·1
9·6	14·0	17·4	15·9	13·6	11·2	11·5
2·5	6·9	10·7	8·8	2·9	4·1	5·4

In the above addition square there are 7 mistakes. One has already been circled. Find the remaining 6 mistakes and put a circle around each one.

Learning objectives

• Quick and accurate addition of pairs of decimal numbers

Guidance notes

Explain to your child how the addition square is made up. For example, the number 11·0, which is ringed, is obtained by adding the number in the left-hand column opposite it (3·7) to the number in the top row directly above it (6·3). Because 3·7 + 6·3 is 10·0 the number 11·0 is ringed. When your child has finished check the ringed numbers with him or her.

More grids

Fill in the missing numbers in the addition and multiplication grids below.

+	9		8
2		6	
7			
	12		

+	5		9	
4		10		
	12	13		
6				13

×	3	2	1
4			
5	15		
3			

×	2	6	10	4
5				
			30	
2				

Learning objectives

• To solve number puzzles, using addition and multiplication facts

Guidance notes

You may need to check that you child remembers how to complete each grid.

A fractional word search

1. $^2/_6$ of 45 is ....

2. How many grams is $^7/_{100}$ of 1 kilogram? ....

3. How many pence is one-sixth of £3? ....

4. $^1/_{100}$ of 800 is ....

5. How many pence is $^{37}/_{100}$ of £2? ....

6. How many days in $^2/_3$ of 3 weeks? ....

7. $^3/_6$ of 54? ....

8. How many £s is $^3/_4$ of £24? ....

9. If I sleep for $^3/_8$ of a day, how many hours do I sleep? ....

10. How many centimetres is $^6/_{10}$ of 1 metre? ....

L	J	H	D	Q	X	T	S	R	D	S	Z	J	F
S	E	V	E	N	T	Y	L	F	G	I	N	M	I
Y	K	T	H	D	L	T	Q	F	O	X	A	E	F
L	O	A	T	Y	S	I	X	I	L	T	S	D	T
F	O	U	R	T	E	E	N	F	L	Y	S	K	E
E	H	S	P	L	V	T	J	T	O	T	E	N	E
E	K	T	H	D	E	K	Q	Y	T	Y	A	L	N
I	A	P	H	S	N	G	R	P	O	X	A	K	N
G	O	S	E	V	E	N	T	Y	F	O	U	R	O
H	F	T	P	E	R	T	Y	L	E	V	R	N	G
T	I	T	W	E	N	T	Y	S	E	V	E	N	S
E	I	G	H	T	E	E	N	P	R	I	E	I	K
N	K	T	H	D	O	Z	Q	K	G	O	A	N	Q
Y	S	I	X	T	Y	S	E	V	E	N	A	E	T

Find the answers to each of the questions above. The answers are written in words in the word search either horizontally or vertically. When you have found the word put a ring around it.

Down and across

Complete the fraction grids by adding the fractions vertically and horizontally. The first one has been done for you.
Example:

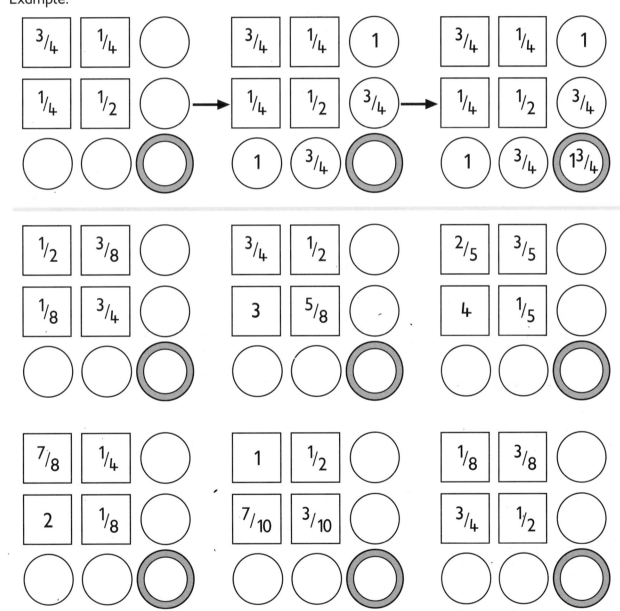

Learning objectives

• To add fractions, including whole numbers, halves, quarters, eighths and tenths.

Guidance notes

You may need to check that your child knows how to complete each section.

You will need
• A pencil and paper

Number chains

Put the number 8 in the start box and follow the arrows in the chain. Every circle contains an instruction (it tells you what to do with your number). You should finish with the number 11 in the answer box.

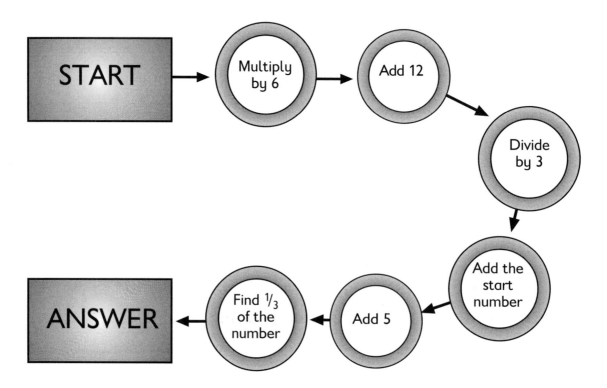

START → Multiply by 6 → Add 12 → Divide by 3 → Add the start number → Add 5 → Find ⅓ of the number → ANSWER

Now try these start numbers:

1.   6 ....

2.   7 ....

3.   1½ ....

4.   2·5 ....

What do you notice about your answers? ....

Learning objectives

• Accurately following a series of instructions involving addition, multiplication, division, fractions and decimals

Guidance notes

You may need to show your child how to complete the number chain by working through with the start number 8. When all four numbers have been tried, talk about the answers and what the possible link is between the start numbers and the answers.

Name

Class   **Date**

You will need
- A pencil and paper
- A die

Roll the dice

Is it true that six is the best number to roll to begin a game because it is more likely to be thrown than the other numbers?

Roll a die fifty times, making a tally chart of the number thrown on your paper.

Fill in your results on the bar line chart below.

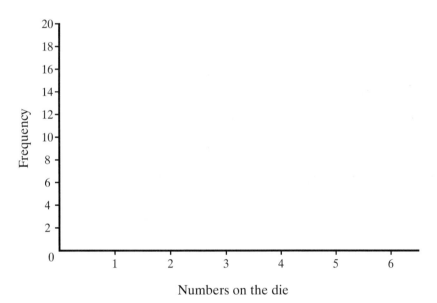

Numbers on the die

1. Was the six the most frequently thrown number? ....

2. If not, which number/s were? ....

3. Do you think you will have the same result next time? ....

4. Why? ....

Take your results to your teacher to be compared with other pupils' results.

Name

Class　　**Date**

You will need
- A pencil and paper for each player
- A die with the numbers from one to six

Making 99

A game for two or more players

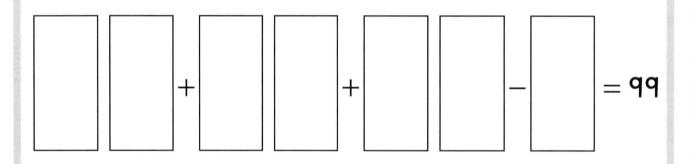

Each player draws the grid, as above, on their paper. Players take it in turns to throw the die. All players put the number thrown in one of the boxes on their grid. The game finishes after the grid has been filled up and the player who makes a total nearest to 99 (above or below) gets one point.

The game is played six more times and the winner is the player who scores most points.

Learning objectives
- Working out a strategy for the best position to place the numbers
- Quick and accurate addition and subtraction of one- and two-digit numbers

Guidance notes

It is helpful if you can play this game with your child.

When each game has finished, encourage your child to check the other players' calculations to ensure they are correct.

Name

Class   **Date**

You will need
• A pencil

What chance?

Match one of these words to each of the statements below.

Certain   Likely   Unlikely   Impossible

• Tomorrow will be hot. ....

• It will rain on Sunday. ....

• I will grow taller than my mother. ....

• It will get dark tonight. ....

• I will see an alien in the garden tonight. ....

In the following sentences, delete a word to make the statement true for you.

• It is likely/unlikely I will watch television tonight.

• It is certain/uncertain that tomorrow I will be older.

• It is possible/impossible/unlikely that it will snow on my birthday.

• There is a good/poor chance of my family winning the lottery.

Write some statements of your own

• It is certain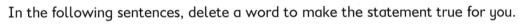

• It is possible that...

• It is impossible that...

• It is unlikely that

• I have no chance of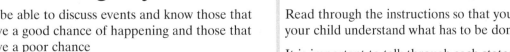

Learning objectives

• To be able to discuss events and know those that have a good chance of happening and those that have a poor chance
Vocabulary: certain, uncertain, likely, unlikely, chance, impossible

Guidance notes

Read through the instructions so that you can help your child understand what has to be done.

It is important to talk through each statement and match it correctly.

You will need
• A pencil and paper

A money puzzle

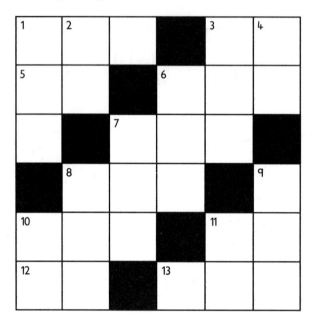

	Across		Down
1	Mabel saved 5p every day in January. By the end of the month she had saved .... p.	1	£141 decreased by £23 gives £ .....
3	How many pencils costing 30p each can I buy for £4?	2	$\frac{1}{4}$ of £2.08 is .... p.
5	20% of £60 is £	3	£6.42 − £5.15 = ... p.
6	$\frac{1}{10}$ of £1,200 is £..........	4	$\frac{1}{100}$ of £30 = ... p.
7	£50 − £42.83 is .... p.	6	50% of £2.36 = ... p.
8	How many pence is £6.28?	7	6 x £1.20 = ... p.
10	£102.93 rounded to the nearest £10 is £......	8	5 twenty pence coins and 10 fifty pence coins make .... p.
11	The difference between £3.47 and £2.68 is ....p.	9	£139 increased by £53 = £ ....
12	$\frac{1}{5}$ of £2.50 is .... p.	10	How many apples costing 20p each can I buy for £3?
13	8 books at 49p each cost .... p.	11	12p + 28p + 39p = ... p

Learning objectives

• Solving number problems using the four rules involving fractions, decimals and percentages

Guidance notes

Explain to your child the answers should be written in figures on the puzzle.

Check the answers when finished and talk about any difficult ones.

You will need
- A pencil
- A ruler

Identify the shape

Using the diagram below answer the following questions and follow the instructions.

1.   Which of these triangles are equilateral? .... Colour them blue.

2.   Which of these triangles are scalene? .... Colour them red.

3.   Which of these triangles are isosceles? .... Colour them yellow.

4.   Which of these triangles have right-angles? ....

5.   Triangle 1 is congruent with which other triangles? ....

6.   Name any other congruent triangles. ....

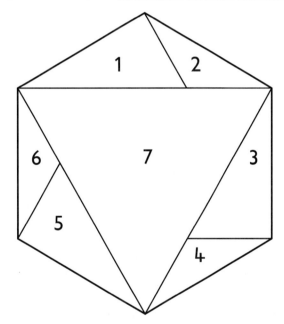

7.   Bisect the equilateral triangle, by drawing a dotted line. Name the properties of the triangles produced. ....

Name

Class   **Date**

You will need
• A pencil

Decimal differences

Can you find two numbers next to each other that have a difference of 2.5? Draw a ring around them. One has already been done for you.

Draw rings around each of the sets of numbers you can find with a difference of 2.5: there should be six sets in total. The sets of numbers may be horizontal, vertical or diagonal.

10·0	7·5	4·0	3·7	6·8	9·1
8·0	4·8	2·6	5·1	7·4	6·6
1·1	4·4	9·1	2·7	1·6	3·4
6·9	1·3	2·4	3·3	3·0	1·8
0·6	5·8	0·9	2·0	0·8	4·3
7·3	4·8	9·4	7·6	9·0	1·3

Learning objectives

• Quick and accurate subtraction of pairs of decimal numbers
• Finding a strategy for eliminating pairs that obviously cannot have the required differences

Guidance notes

Encourage your child to set a challenge of finding the numbers as quickly as possible.

When your child has finished check the ringed pairs of numbers and show him or her any that were missed.

You will need
• A pencil and paper

Making numbers

4   8   12

Using the numbers 4, 8, and 12 and any of the operations +, −, ×, ÷, how many different numbers can you make in 20 minutes? You must use all three numbers each time. Put your numbers in order starting with the smallest one. You can use fractions and negative numbers. Write your answers here:

Learning objectives

• Addition, subtraction, multiplication and division of one- and two-digit numbers
• Simple fractions
• Ordering numbers including negatives numbers and fractions

Vocabulary: operation, negative

Guidance notes

Encourage your child to try and include with their list fractions and negative numbers. For example:
$^4/_8 + 12 = 12^1/_2$ and $8 − 12 − 4 = −8$

When your child has finished, check the answers and talk about any that are incorrect. A common mistake is to think that −4 is less than −8.

Name

Class   **Date**

You will need
- A large sheet of squared paper
- A mirror
- A pencil
- A ruler

Growing symmetry

On a large piece of paper draw this shape.

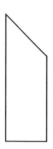

Choose one of the sides to be the mirror line for your pattern and draw the reflection.

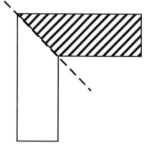

Now do the same again choosing a different side of the shape.

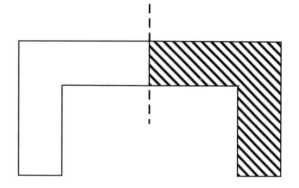

Continue growing your pattern until you run out of space!

Could you have made a bigger pattern if you had used different mirror lines?

Learning objectives

- To recognise where a shape will be reflected in a mirror line parallel to one side

Guidance notes

You may need to make sure your child positions the mirror carefully to check the reflected shape and to draw it accurately.

Name

Class   **Date**

You will need
• A pencil

What's the number?

I am a two-digit number.
I am a multiple of 7.
If I add my digits they make a total of 6.
What number am I? _____

I am a two-digit number less than 30.
I am an odd number.
The difference between my digits is 5.
What number am I? _____

I am a prime number.
I am less than 20
The product of my digits is 7.
What number am I? _____

I am a two-digit number.
I am a multiple of 11.
The difference between my digits is 0.
The sum of my digits is 12.
What number am I?

_____

I am a two-digit number.
I am an odd number.
The sum of my digits is 12.
The units digit is three times bigger than the tens digit.
What number am I?

_____

I am a square number less than 100 but more than 50.
I am not an even number.
What number am I? _____

Make up some puzzles of your own.

Learning objectives

• To solve simple word problems

Guidance notes

Talk to your child about the strategies he or she uses for solving each puzzle.

You will need
• A pencil and paper

A measurement puzzle

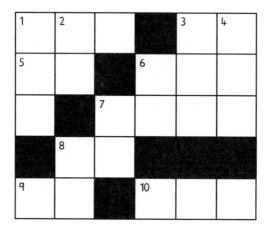

	Across		Down
1	A jug contains 365ml of milk. If I add another 250ml how many ml will now be in the jug?	1	One piece of string is 325cm long. How many cm long are two pieces?
3	Dad's van holds 63 litres of petrol. It is $\frac{1}{3}$ full. How many litres is this?	2	$\frac{1}{10}$ of 1 metre = ... cm
5	How many minutes in $\frac{5}{6}$ of 1 hour?	3	How many degrees are there in $\frac{3}{4}$ of a turn?
6	30cm less than 2m = ... cm	4	A square has each side 25cm. How many cm is its perimeter?
7	I have six puppies each weighing 450gm. How many gm do all six weigh?	6	A large container holds 34 litres. It is half full. How many litres is this?
8	A piece of wood 720cm long is cut into ten equal pieces. How many cm long is each piece?	7	One bag of flour weighs 2·2kg. How many kg do ten bags weigh?
9	A TV programme starts at 14.30 and finishes at 15.25. How many minutes does it last?	8	How many years in $\frac{3}{4}$ of a century?
10	A train leaves Bristol at 7.30 a.m. and arrives in London at 9.15 a.m. How many minutes does the journey take?		

Learning objectives

• Solving number problems involving measurement of capacity, length, mass and also time

Guidance notes

Explain to your child the answers should be written in figures on the puzzle.

Check the answers when finished and talk about any difficult ones.

Name

Class   Date

You will need
• A pencil and paper

Number chains

Choose a number.
If it is an odd number multiply it by 3 and add 1.
If it is an even number divide it by 2.
Follow these rules for each new number until you reach 1.

If I choose 20 as my starting number, the chain would look like this:

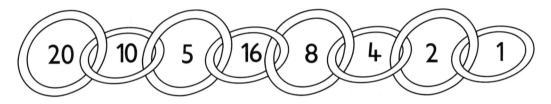

20   10   5   16   8   4   2   1

Continue the number chains for these numbers:

21 → 64 → __ → __ → __ → __ → __ → __ → __ → __

13 → __ → __ → __ → __ → __ → __ → __ → __ → __

6 → __ → __ → __ → __ → __ → __ → __ → __ → __

Make all the number chains for the numbers up to 20.
Do you need to do all of them? ....
What do you notice about the patterns you have made?

....
....
....
....

Learning objectives

• To recognise odd and even numbers
• To solve number puzzles

Guidance notes

You may need to help your child follow the instructions to complete a number chain.

Factors, factors, factors

A game for two players

8	12	15	16	18
24	30	36	40	44
48	50	56	60	64
66	70	72	78	80
85	86	90	94	100

Each player throws a die to decide who starts. The player throwing the highest number starts. Players take it in turns to throw the two dice. The numbers on the two dice are added together, and if this number is a factor of one of the numbers on the grid the player puts one of his or her coloured counters on that number. When all the numbers have been covered the player with most counters on the grid is the winner. The game is played again with the second player starting.

| Name |
| Class | Date |

You will need
- A pencil
- Scissors
- Squared paper

Which will make an open cube?

Here are different nets that might make an open cube (a cube without a top or lid). Make them out of squared paper. Put a tick by those that will make a cube and a cross by those that will not.

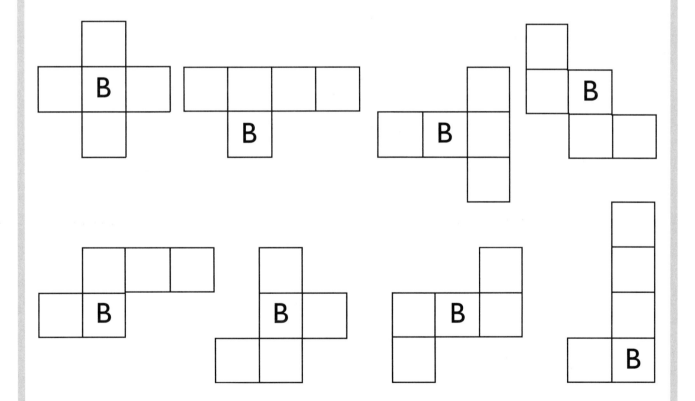

Learning objectives

- To be able to identify the nets that will make an open cube

Vocabulary: identify

Guidance notes

Read through the instructions so that you can help your child understand what has to be done.

You may have to help your child with folding the paper to make the cube.

You will need
• A pencil
• Blunt scissors
• Paper

Which angle is it?

Make a right-angle marker out of any scrap of paper.

Using a pair of scissors open the blade to 90 degrees, checking with the angle marker.

An acute angle is less than a right angle: between 0 and 90 degrees.
Using the pair of scissors, close the blade slightly: the angle should be an acute one.
Draw, using the scissors, three other acute angles on this page.

An obtuse angle is more than a right angle but less than a straight line – between 90 and 180 degrees.
Using the pair of scissors, open the blade wider than a right angle, checking with the angle marker that the angle is an obtuse one.
Draw, using the scissors, three other obtuse angles on this page.

Learning objectives

• To be able to identify and draw acute and obtuse angles
Vocabulary: identify, acute, obtuse

Guidance notes

Read through the instructions so that you can help your child understand what has to be done.

Allow your child to complete each part before reading the next instruction.

You may have to help him or her with folding the paper to make the right angle marker.

Name

Class　　　　**Date**

Mental maths quiz 1

1. Kate saved 25p a week for 20 weeks. How much did she save in total?

   ....

2. Fill in the spaces in this grid:

Fraction	Decimal	Percentage
¼		
	0·3	
		20%

3. Write 27,845 in words. ....

4. Give a number that has factors of 1, 2, 3 and 4. ....

5. 7·5m is .... centimetres.

6. Round 8315 to the nearest 1000, the nearest 100 and the nearest 10. ....

7. What is $^3/_{10}$ of £40? ....

8. If the temperature was −3°C at 6:00 a.m. and 7°C at 12:00 noon, how many degrees did the temperature rise? ....

9. What is 309×10? ....

10. If 1 is the first square number, what is the sixth? ....

11. Give the next two numbers in this sequence: −30, −24, −18, __ , __ .

12. What number is halfway between 36,400 and 37,000? ....

13. What is $678 − 108$? Explain how you worked it out. ....

    ....

14. Which of these angles is acute and which obtuse?

    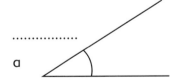　　　　

    ....　　　　　...............　　　　...............

    a　　　　　　　　　b　　　　　　　c

15. What do we call lines that are always the same distance apart? ....

Learning objectives

- To revise a range of mathematical topics

Guidance notes

The answers can be written in the spaces provided. Your child will need a pencil and may wish to use a calculator for this exercise.

Mental maths quiz 2

1. Pens cost 30p: how much would you pay for nine of them? ....

2. Fill in the spaces in this grid:

Fraction	Decimal	Percentage
$\frac{1}{5}$		
	0·25	
		40%

3. Write 83,217 in words. ....

4. Give a multiple of 9 between 80 and 100. ....

5. How many grams in 2·5kg? ....

6. Round 92,056 to the nearest 1000, the nearest 100 and the nearest 10. ....

7. What is $^3/_4$ of £60? ....

8. If the temperature was –8°C at midnight and 7°C at noon how many degrees did the temperature rise? ....

9. What is 462×100? ....

10. If 1 is the first square number, what is the sum of the third and fourth square numbers? ....

11. Give the next two numbers in this sequence: $1^1/_4$, $1^1/_2$, $1^3/_4$, ..., ...

12. What is 11×45? Explain how you worked it out. ....
....

13. What do we call a shape that has ten sides? ....

14. What is half of 676? ....

15. What do we call lines that are at right angles to each other?

    For example: _____   ....

Learning objectives

• To revise a range of mathematical topics

Guidance notes

The answers can be written in the spaces provided.
Your child will need a pencil and may wish to use a
calculator for this exercise.

Mental maths quiz 3

1. Petrol costs 83.7p per litre. How much would you pay for 10 litres? ....

2. Fill in the spaces in this grid:

Fraction	Decimal	Percentage
$^{11}/_{20}$		
	0·75	
		1%

3. Write 605 416 in words. ....

4. Give all the factors of 24. ....

5. How many millilitres in 3 litres? ....

6. Round 123 358 to the nearest 10 000, 1000, the nearest 100 and the nearest 10.

    ....

7. What is $^{2}/_{3}$ of £105? ....

8. If in five minutes of play you moved your score on a video game from −3400 to 5500: how many points have you scored in those five minutes? ....

9. 378 × .... = 37 800?

10. If 1 is the first square number, what is the difference between the fourth and sixth square numbers? ....

11. Give the next two numbers in this sequence: 1·75, 2, 2·25, ... , ...

12. What number is halfway between −24 and 36? ....

13. What is 111 × 30? Explain how you worked it out. ....

    ....

14. What do we call a shape that has six identical square faces? ....

15. What do we call triangles that have three equal angles and three sides of the same length? ....

Learning objectives

- To revise a range of mathematical topics

Guidance notes

The answers can be written in the spaces provided. Your child will need a pencil and may wish to use a calculator for this exercise.

Mental maths quiz 4

1.   If 10 tickets for the cinema cost £23, how much does one cost? ....

2.   Fill in the spaces in this grid:

Fraction	Decimal	Percentage
$^2/_5$		
	0·01	
		10%

3.   Write 725 725 in words. ....

4.   Give a multiple of 12 that is between 125 and 144. ....

5.   How many millimetres in 30 centimetres? ....

6.   Round these numbers to the nearest whole number: 7·2, 8·5, 4·6. ....

7.   What is $^2/_5$ of £105? ....

8.   423 × .... = 4230?

9.   Give the next two numbers in this sequence: 4, 2, 0, ..., ...

10. What number is halfway between −54 and 46? ....

11. What is 6·5 + 8·3? Explain how you worked it out. ....
     ....

12. What do we call a shape that has four identical triangular faces?
     ....

13. What is double 125·5? ....

14. What do we call triangles that have two equal sides and
     two equal angles? ....

15. I have read 125 pages of a book that has 360 pages. How many more pages must I
     read to get to the middle of the book? ....

Learning objectives

• To revise a range of mathematical topics

Guidance notes

The answers can be written in the spaces provided.
Your child will need a pencil and may wish to use a
calculator for this exercise.

Mental maths quiz 5

1. How many weeks would it take to save £30.00 if I save £1.50 each week? ....

2. Fill in the spaces in this grid:

Fraction	Decimal	Percentage
$^4/_5$		
	0·15	
		16%

3. Write 1 400 000 in words. ....

4. Write down all the factors of 36 that are even numbers. ....

5. How many square millimetres in a square centimetre? ....

6. Round 151·8 to the nearest 100, the nearest 10 and the
    nearest whole number. ....

7. What is 30% of £120? ....

8. 7900 ÷ .... = 79?

9. Give the next two numbers in this sequence: 2·3, 3·0, 3·7,........ , ...

10. What number is halfway between 18 500 and 26 500? ....

11. What must you take from 225 to leave 55? Explain how you worked it out. ....

12. Give the name of a 3D shape that has only 1 face. ....

13. What is double 2·6?...

14. What is the area and perimeter of a square with sides of 8cm?

    ....

15. A TV programme starts at 14:45 and ends at 15:25: how long is the programme?

    ....

Learning objectives

- To revise a range of mathematical topics

Guidance notes

The answers can be written in the spaces provided. Your child will need a pencil and may wish to use a calculator for this exercise.

Mental maths quiz 6

1. How many exercise books costing 60p could I buy with £5? ....

2. Fill in the spaces in this grid:

Fraction	Decimal	Percentage
$^{1}/_{100}$		
	0·45	
		65%

3. Write 1 726 138 in words. ....

4. Write down all the factors of 60 that are odd numbers. ....

5. How many square centimetres in a square metre? ....

6. Round 235·5 to the nearest 100, the nearest 10 and the nearest whole number ....

7. What is 75% of £120? ....

8. 42 000 ÷ .... = 4200?

9. Give the next two numbers in this sequence: 4, 0, –4, ... , ...

10. What number is halfway between 3·6 and 5·4? ....

11. What must you take from 375 to leave 265? Explain how you worked it out.

    ....

12. Give the name of a 3D shape that has only 3 faces. ....

13. What is double 15·7? ....

14. What is the perimeter of a regular octagon with sides of 8cm? ....

15. A film starts at 19:25 and ends at 21:10: how long is the film?

    ....

Learning objectives

- To revise a range of mathematical topics

Guidance notes

The answers can be written in the spaces provided. Your child will need a pencil and may wish to use a calculator for this exercise.

Money problems

1. In the multipacks how much do you pay for 1 pencil? ....

2. In the multipacks how much do you pay for 1 rubber? ....

3. In the multipacks how much do you pay for 1 pen? ....

4. In the multipacks how much do you pay for 1 sheet of coloured paper? ....

5. In the multipacks how much do you pay for 1 envelope? ....

6. If you bought 25 pencils in multipacks instead of as individual items how much would you save? ....

7. If you bought 30 rubbers in multipacks instead of as individual items how much would you save? ....

8. If you bought 500 sheets of coloured paper in multipacks instead of as individual items how much would you save? ....

9. If you bought 250 envelopes in multipacks instead of as individual items how much would you save? ....

10. If you bought 32 pens in multipacks instead of as individual items how much would you save? ....

Learning objectives

• Solve problems involving money

Guidance notes

The answers can be written in the spaces provided. Your child will need a pencil and may wish to use a calculator for this exercise.

Looking at graphs

The time of a journey taken for a school sponsored walk

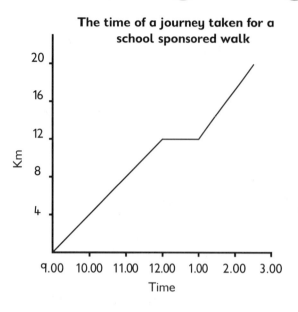

The colour of sweets in a packet

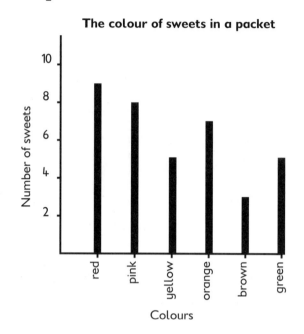

Using the bar line graph:

1.   Which colour sweet is the most common? ....

2.   How many brown sweets were there? ....

3.   How many more red sweets than yellow sweets were there? ....

4.   Which two colours have the same number of sweets in the pack? ....

5.   How many sweets were there in the packet? ....

Using the line graph:

6.   How far did the children walk? ....

7.   About what time was it when they finished the walk? ....

8.   What do you think might have happened between 12:00 and 1:00?

     ....

9.   Approximately how long did the walk take? ....

10. Approximately what time was it when they reached the halfway point in the walk?

     ....

Learning objectives

• Solve a problem by interpreting data in graphs
Vocabulary: bar line graph, line graph

Guidance notes

The answers can be written in the spaces provided.
Your child will need a pencil.

Square numbers

Square numbers are made by multiplying a number by itself. The first three square numbers are 1 (1 × 1), 4 (2 × 2) and 9 (3 × 3). They are called square because they are numbers that, if represented by counters, could be arranged as a square.

For example, 2 × 2:

3 × 3:

1. Tell me the first ten square numbers (the first three are written above).

   ....

2. What is the eleventh square number? ....

3. If we arranged some tiles in a square, and we know that there were 12 tiles along one edge, how many tiles would there be altogether? ....

4. Which of these numbers is not a square number: 81, 100, 42 and 36? ....

5. How many centimetre squares would there be on a square piece of paper with sides of 1 metre? ....

6. What is $2^2 + 4^2$? ....

7. What is $2^2 + 6^2$? ....

8. What is $4^2 + 8^2$? ....

9. Which two square numbers can be added together to make the fifth square number?

   ....

10. Which two square numbers can be added together to make the tenth square number?

    ....

Learning objectives

- To recognise square numbers
Vocabulary: square numbers

Guidance notes

The answers can be written in the spaces provided. Your child will need a pencil and may wish to use a calculator for this exercise.

Decimal numbers

Class	Money collected in sponsored swim
1	£4.37
2	£15.05
3	£13.50
4	£7.79
5	£21.12

	Distances jumped in long jump
Jack	5·72m
Melanie	3·50m
Tyson	4·27m
Patrick	3·97m
Ranjit	5·52m

Children's heights	
Amy	1.52m
Bilal	1.60m
Jack	1.48m
George	1.62m
Helen	1.50m
Maria	1.55m
Sunita	1.59m
Peter	1.57m

1. Put the classes into descending order of how much they collected in the sponsored swim.

    ....

2. Put the children into descending order for the distance they jumped in the long jump.

    ....

3. Put the children in ascending order of their heights.

    ....

4. Give the amount each class collected in the sponsored swim to the nearest £1.

    ....

5. Give the length of each child's long jump to the nearest metre.

    ....

6. Give each child's height to the nearest 10cm.

    ....

Learning objectives

- To order sets of decimal numbers
- To round decimals to the nearest whole number

Vocabulary: to the nearest whole number, ascending order, descending order

Guidance notes

Before starting the questions you might first want to check that your child understands what each table is showing.

Read the questions/instructions and ask your child for the answers.

Name

Class   Date

Fractions

A	B	C	D
50	20	£1	£1.20
20	32	£5	£2
100	100	£10	£3.60

1. What is $3/10$ of each of the numbers in column A? ...., ..., ...

2. What is $3/4$ of each of the numbers in column B? ...., ..., ...

3. What is $3/5$ of each of the amounts in column C? ...., ..., ...

4. What is $3/4$ of each of the amounts in column D? ...., ..., ...

5. What is $7/10$ of each of the numbers in column A? ...., ..., ...

6. What is $9/10$ of each of the numbers in column A? ...., ..., ...

7. What is $2/5$ of each of the amounts in column C? ...., ..., ...

8. What is $3/4$ of each of the amounts in column C? ...., ..., ...

9. What is $3/10$ of each of the amounts in columns C and D? ...., ..., ...,
    ...., ..., ...

10. What is $6/10$ of each of the amounts in columns C and D? ...., ..., ...,
    ...., ..., ...

Learning objectives

• To find fractional amounts of numbers and money

Guidance notes

The answers can be written in the spaces provided.
Your child will need a pencil.

Area and perimeter

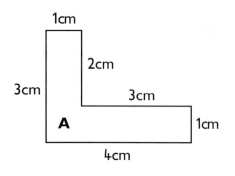

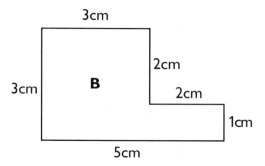

1. What would be the area of shape A? ....

2. What would be the perimeter of shape A? ....

3. What would be the area of shape B? ....

4. What would be the perimeter of shape B? ....

5. What would be the area and perimeter of a square with sides of 11mm? ....
   ....

6. What would be the area and perimeter of a square with sides of 15m? ....
   ....

7. What would be the area and perimeter of a football pitch if it was 80 metres long and 50 metres wide? ....

8. What would be the area and perimeter of a rectangular swimming pool that had a length of 25m and a width of 12m? ....

9. Choose the most likely area for a £5 note:

   95cm²   9·5m²   950m²   95mm²

10. Choose the most likely area for a kitchen floor:

    12cm²   12m²   200m²   120mm²

Learning objectives

- Measure and calculate the area and perimeter of simple shapes
Vocabulary: m², square metres, mm², square millimetres

Guidance notes

The answers can be written in the spaces provided. Your child will need a pencil.

Name

Class   **Date**

Factors

A factor is a whole number that will divide exactly into another whole number. For example, 6 is a factor of 30 because 30 ÷ 6 = 5. 1, 2, 3, 5, 10, 15 and 30 itself are also factors of 30.

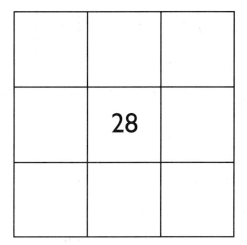

	28	

| 35 | 42 | 54 | 15 | 27 | 49 | 56 | 40 |

Select numbers from this list and follow the instructions to put them on to the grid.

1.   Put the number that only has 1, 7 and itself as factors in the space under 28.

2.   Put the number for which 9 is a factor but 2 is not in the space to the left of 28.

3.   Put the number that has both 3 and 7 as factors in the space above 28.

4.   Put the number that has both 5 and 3 as factors in the space below 27.

5.   Put the number that has both 5 and 7 as factors in the space to the right of 28.

6.   Put the number that has both 8 and 5 as factors in the space above 35.

7.   Put the number that has 2, 3, 6 and 9 as factors in the space above 27.

8.   Put the number that has both 7 and 8 as factors in the last space.

Learning objectives

- Identify the factors of numbers
Vocabulary: factor

Guidance notes

Read the instructions and ask your child to complete the grid. Your child will need a pencil.

Percentages

Row 1	100	50	200
Row 2	15	25	20
Row 3	16	20	24
Row 4	32	44	36
Row 5	£1	£2	£10

1.   What is 50% of each of the numbers in the first row? ....

2.   What is 10% of each of the numbers in the first row? ....

3.   What is 20% of each of the numbers in the first row? ....

4.   What is 50% of each of the numbers in row 3? ....

5.   What is 25% of each of the numbers in row 3? ....

6.   What is 50% of each of the numbers in row 4? ....

7.   What is 75% of each of the numbers in row 4? ....

8.   What is 75% of each of the amounts in row 5? ....

9.   What is 25% of each of the amounts in row 5? ....

10. What is 20% of each of the amounts in row 5? ....

Learning objectives

• Find percentages of numbers or quantities
Vocabulary: percentage

Guidance notes

Read the questions/instruction and ask your child to answer.

Number puzzles

Use the clues to find the numbers

The first number is a two-digit multiple of 7. The sum of the two digits is 3.	The second number is an odd two-digit multiple of 9. The product of the two digits is 14.	Find three numbers that are two-digit multiples of 6. For each number the sum of the two digits is 6. ....
Find a two-digit multiple of 7 for which the product of the two digits is a multiple of 10.	Find three two-digit multiples of 8 for which the product of the two digits are also multiples of 8.	Find two two-digit multiples of 9 for which the difference between the two digits is 5. ....
Find a three-digit number. All the digits are even. The hundreds digit is half the tens digit. The units digit is double the tens digit.	Find a three-digit number. All the digits are odd. The units digit is three times as big as the hundreds digit. The tens digit is three times as big as the units digit.	Another three-digit number The units digit is the largest. The sum of the three digits is 6. Each digit is different. The hundreds digit is the smallest. ....
	The last number is a three-digit number. The sum of the digits is 16. The hundreds and units digit are the same and both odd. The tens digit is smaller than the other two.	

Learning objectives

• To solve mathematical puzzles
Vocabulary: digits, multiples, sum, product, difference

Guidance notes

Read the questions/instructions and ask your child to answer. Your child will need a pencil.

Glossary

There are a large number of words and phrases that your child needs to understand and use if he or she is to make good progress in mathematics. Already in Years 1, 2, 3 and 4 many commonly used terms have been introduced and they will continue to be used in Year 5. In addition, there are a number of additional words and phrases that your child may meet for the first time.

The words and phrases listed below are some of those most commonly used and they will be introduced and used continually by teachers in their lessons at school – it will be helpful if you could refer to them at the appropriate times in your home environment. If there are some that still appear to cause confusion it would greatly assist your child's understanding if you could explain their meanings. To assist, where necessary, an explanation of some of the words has been incorporated.

Numbers and calculations

ascending/descending order

Formula – a quick way of writing a rule: e.g. area = length × width or A = l × w

Factor – whole numbers that divide exactly into another number: e.g. 2 is a factor of 6

Square number – the number you get when you multiply a number by itself: e.g. 4 = 2 × 2 (so 4 is a square number)

Percentage

Exchange rate

Currency

Number sentence: e.g. 4 + 3 = 7

Handling data

Line graph – uses lines to join up points on a graph: temperature changes, for example

Bar line graph – similar to a bar chart but using lines

Likely, unlikely

Certain

Possible, impossible

No chance

Measures, shape and space

Square metre

Square millimetre

24-hour clock

12-hour clock

Congruent – shapes are congruent if they are identical to each other in shape and size

Octahedron – a 3D shape with 8 faces

Scalene triangle – a triangle having no equal sides

Parallel – lines that stay the same distance apart; they can be straight or curved

Quadrant – a special sector that is one quarter of a circle

Acute angle – a turn that is less than 90 degrees

Obtuse angle – a turn that is more than 90 degrees and less than 180 degrees

Bisect – cut into two equal parts

Identify

Answers

Word search 3, 81, 36, 7, 90, 40, 24, 38, 56, 95, 62.

Empty boxes 11 + 4 + 2, 7 – 4 + 11 or 11 – 4 + 7, 11 + 4 – 2, 7 + 4 + 2, 7 – 2 + 4 or 11 – 4 + 2, 7 + 4 – 11, 9 + 2 – 4, 9 + 7 + 4, 9 – 7 + 4, 7 + 4 – 9, 4 + 9 + 2, 7 – 4 + 9

27 mistakes

×	2	3	4	5	6	7	8	9	10
2	4	6	8	⑨	⑪	⑬	16	18	20
3	6	9	⑩	15	18	21	㉓	27	30
4	8	⑪	16	20	24	28	32	㉟	40
5	10	⑭	20	㉔	30	㊱	40	㊹	50
6	12	⑲	24	30	36	42	48	(53)	60
7	14	⑳	28	㊱	42	㊽	56	(62)	70
8	16	㉕	32	㊶	㊾	(55)	64	(71)	80
9	18	27	㉟	45	54	63	(71)	81	90
10	20	30	40	㊺	㊿	(60)	80	90	100

How big is your name? Mary = 57, Jean = 30, Ali = 22. Check your child's answers to 4, 5.

Number search Check your child's number sentences

Making numbers
Check your child's answers.

Make 50p Check your child's answers.

A difference square

–	66	14	9	53	32	48	20
84	⑯	70	75	31	52	㊳	64
8	58	6	1	㊼	㉖	40	12
71	5	(85)	62	18	㊲	23	51
21	45	7	12	㉞	11	㊲	1
50	16	36	41	3	㉘	2	㊵
14	52	㉘	5	39	18	34	6
36	30	22	27	㉗	4	12	16

Is it the same shape? Game

Adding to 27 Game

Estimating and measuring 1 Check your child's estimates and measurement.

Number chains 4, 3·5, 4·5, 5·5

Guess the shape Game

Make it big Game

Estimating and measuring 2 Check your child's estimates and measurements.

Dart to 50 Check your child's combinations making 50.

Shape up Parallelogram, rhombus, star, square, kite, hexagon, octagon, triangle.

Take two 37 +53 = 90, 66 – 37 = 29, 41 + 53 = 94, 21 + 16 = 37, 66 – 25 = 41 66 – 29 = 37

Two missing numbers 7, 6; 3, 12; 7, 20; 10, 17; 11, 15; 23, 25

Making 88 Check your child's answers.

Number puzzles 1) 29, 2) 75, 3) 8, 4) 100, 5) 55, 6) 2

Cross number puzzle

[1] 3	[2] 3	6	■	[3] 3	[4] 4
[5] 9	6	■	[6] 2	3	5
0	■	[7] 1	1	0	■
■	[8] 5	0	6	■	[9] 1
[10] 1	0	2	■	[11] 5	0
[12] 2	0	■	[13] 1	0	7

Consecutive numbers 56 = 7 × 8, 72 = 9 × 8, 240 = 16 × 15, 420 = 20 × 21, 702 = 26 × 27, 1406 = 37 × 38
60 = 3 × 4 × 5, 504 = 7 × 8 × 9,
1320 = 10 × 11 × 12, 2184 = 12 × 13 × 14
10 626 = 21 × 22 × 23

Hitting the target 14 +17 +19, 12 + 14 + 19, 14 + 19 – 17, 12 + 14 – 19, 14 – 12 + 19, 19 + 17 – 12

Smallest amount of coins
Row 2: 2, 2, 3, 3, 2, 3, 3, 4, 4, 1
Row 3: 2, 2, 3, 3, 2, 3, 3, 4, 4, 2
Row 4: 3, 3, 4, 4, 3, 4, 4, 5, 5, 2
Row 5: 3, 3, 4, 4, 3, 4, 4, 5, 5, 1
Most coins: 38, 39, 48, 49
Six coins: 88, 89, 98, 99

Mind the gap 25 + 36 = 61, 29 – 18 = 11, 28 + 30 = 58, 34 + 77 = 111, 16 + 65 = 81 100 – 33 = 67, 123 – 32 = 91, 103 – 44 = 59

Perpendicular Check your child's answers.

An addition square

+	16	22	31	45	38	19	9	44
25	41	47	56	70	63	(54)	34	69
14	30	㊻	45	59	(62)	33	23	58
33	49	55	64	(68)	71	52	㊹	77
46	62	68	(67)	91	84	65	55	90
9	25	31	40	54	㊾	28	18	53
40	56	(72)	71	85	78	59	49	84
37	㉝	59	68	82	75	(66)	46	(71)
23	39	45	(53)	68	61	㊶	32	67

Parallel
Check your child's answers.

A mathematical word search
19, 4, 46, 30, 18, 72, 51, 67, 20, 93, 5

Find the areas Check your child's answers

Number chains 8, 11, 13, 3·5

Fill the gaps

+	14	29
11	25	40
13	27	42

×	6	7
9	54	63
8	48	56

+	15	9	27	32
19	34	28	46	51
27	42	36	54	59
34	49	43	61	66
45	60	54	72	77

×	9	8	6	7
5	45	40	30	35
7	63	56	42	49
9	81	72	54	63
6	54	48	36	42

Making 100 Game

Fraction triangles

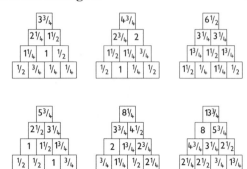

Check the grids your child has made up.

Making numbers Check your child's answers.

Symmetry Check your child's folds and shapes.

Making 99 Check your child's answers.

Measure to the nearest millimetre Check your child's measurements and calculations.

Bingo Game

Travelling times

From home to...	Leaving time	Return time	Time away from home
Zoo	09.00	13.30	4hr 30min
Park	16.30	17.45	1hr 15min
Sports centre	18.15	19.35	1hr 20min
School	08.35	15.50	7hr 15min
Visiting friends	16.40	11.30	18hr 50min
Swimming pool	09.25	11.15	1hr 50min
Shops	10.20	12.50	2hr 30min

Hitting the target

$17 + 23 + 28 = 68$, $28 + 32 + 41 = 101$
$17 + 23 + 32 = 72$, $17 + 28 + 32 = 77$
$23 + 28 + 32 = 83$, $23 + 32 + 41 = 96$

Number routes Check your child's answers and discuss the results.

4, 4, 4, 4 Check your child's answers.

Finding smaller areas Check your child's measurements and calculations.

Number sequences in a square

124	118	112	106	100	94	88	82	76	70	64
1·2	1·4	1·6	1·8	2·0	2·2	2·4	2·6	2·8	3·0	58
11	22	33	44	55	66	77	88	99	3·2	52
96	91	86	81	76	71	66	61	110	3·4	46
100	110	120	130	140	150	160	56	121	3·6	40
3	7	11	15	19	23	170	51	132	3·8	34
6	12	18	24	30	27	180	46	143	4·0	28
3	6	9	12	36	31	190	41	154	4·2	22
2	4	6	15	42	35	200	36	165	4·4	16
		8	18	48	39	210	31	176	4·6	10
		10	21	54	43	220	26	187	4·8	4

Measuring in tenths of a litre Check your child's estimates and measuring.

Darting doubles Check your child's combinations.

Odds and evens

10, 12, 14, 16; 9, 11, 13, 15;
12, 16, 64, 184, 320 – all even
8, 52, 70, 192, 306 – all even

+	EVEN	ODD
EVEN	even	odd
ODD	odd	even

×	EVEN	ODD
EVEN	even	even
ODD	even	odd

A number puzzle

¹1	²5	0	■	³1	⁴7
⁵4	0	■	⁶6	7	5
8	■	⁷1	3	0	■
■	⁸1	0	0	■	⁹1
¹⁰2	5	8	■	¹¹1	2
¹²9	0	■	¹³4	8	0

School timetable

ACTIVITY	START TIME	DIGITAL TIME	24HOUR TIME
START SCHOOL	Five to nine in the morning	8.55 a.m.	08:55
ASSEMBLY	Quarter past nine in the morning	9.15 a.m.	09:15
LITERACY HOUR	Twenty-five to ten in the morning	9.35 a.m.	09:35
BREAKTIME	Twenty to eleven in the morning	10.40 a.m.	10:40
NUMERACY HOUR	Eleven o'clock in the morning	11.00 a.m.	11:00
LUNCHTIME	Ten past twelve	12.10 p.m.	12:10
START OF AFTERNOON	Twenty past one in the afternoon	1.20 p.m.	13:20
END OF SCHOOL TIME	A quarter to four in the afternoon	3.45 p.m.	15:45
AFTER-SCHOOL CLUB	Four o'clock in the afternoon	4.00 p.m.	16:00
SCHOOL MEETING FOR PARENTS	Half past seven in the evening	7.30 p.m.	19:30

1. 20 minutes, 2. 1 hour 10 minutes, 3. 2 hours 25 minutes, 4. 4.45 p.m. or 16:45, 5. 9.20 p.m. or 21:20

Mind the gap $37 + 45 = 82$, $33 − 14 = 19$, $47 + 31 = 78$, $67 + 37 = 104$, $25 + 58 = 83$, $100 − 76 = 24$, $109 − 41 = 68$, $111 − 36 = 75$

Measuring in tenths of a kilogram Check your child's estimates and measurements.

Decimal sums

2·6	2·7	1·6	6·2	9·4	5·1
5·7	4·0	3·4	2·2	6·6	3·3
2·2	0·8	3·0	5·2	7·1	7·2
6·6	1·8	9·0	3·9	8·0	0·6
1·6	8·4	3·0	1·5	4·5	4·0
0·5	7·9	7·0	1·4	0·9	3·1

Daily temperatures Darwin 25°C, Cape Town 15°C, Hong Kong 13°C, Christchurch 12°C, Athens 6°C, London 2°C, Washington –1°C, Moscow –14°C Check your child's temperatures on the thermometer.
1. 11°C, 2. 8°C, 3. 8°C

Making numbers Check your child's answers for accuracy.

Tree diagram
B) 6, 12, 18, 24, C) 10, 20, D) 2, 4, 8, 14, 16, 22, E) 15, F) 3, 9, 21, G) 5, 25, H) 1, 7, 11, 13, 17, 19, 23, 1) 15, 2) 5, 25, 3) C, E, A, G

A decimal addition square

+	4·4	7·8	6·3	0·4	1·6	2·9
1·6	6·0	9·6	7·9	2·0	3·2	4·5
0·8	5·2	8·6	7·1	1·2	2·4	10·9
3·7	8·1	11·5	11·0	4·1	5·3	6·6
5·2	9·6	14·0	11·5	5·6	6·8	8·1
9·6	14·0	17·4	15·9	13·6	11·2	11·5
2·5	6·9	10·7	8·8	2·9	4·1	5·4

More grids

+	9	4	8
2	11	6	10
7	16	11	15
3	12	7	11

+	5	6	9	7
4	9	10	13	11
7	12	13	16	14
6	11	12	15	13

×	3	2	1
4	12	8	4
5	15	10	5
3	9	6	3

×	2	6	10	4
5	10	30	50	20
3	6	18	30	12
2	4	12	20	8

A fractional word search
15, 70, 50, 8, 74, 14, 27, 18, 9, 60

Down and across

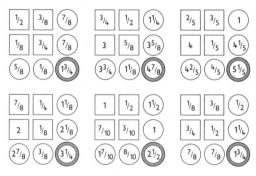

Check your child's 'made-up' grids.

Number chains
9, 10, 4·5, 5·5 The answer is 3 more than the start number.

Roll the dice
Check your child's drawing of the bar line chart.

Making 99 Game

What chance?
Check the accuracy of your child's statements.

A money puzzle

¹1	⁵5	5	■	³1	³3
⁵1	2	■	⁶1	2	0
8	■	⁷7	1	7	■
■	⁸6	2	8	■	⁹1
¹⁰1	0	0	■	⁷9	9
⁵5	0	■	³3	9	2

Identify the shape 1) 7, 2) 1, 3, 5, 3) 2, 4, 6, 4) 1, 3, 5, 5) 3, 5, 6) 2, 4, 6, 7) Scalene; right-angled; congruent

Decimal differences

10·0	7·5	4·0	3·7	6·8	9·1
8·0	4·8	2·6	5·1	7·4	6·6
1·1	4·4	9·1	2·7	1·6	3·4
6·9	1·3	2·4	3·3	3·0	1·8
0·6	5·8	0·9	2·0	0·8	4·3
7·3	4·8	9·4	7·6	9·0	1·3

Making numbers
Check your child's answers for accuracy.

Growing symmetry Discuss the patterns your child has drawn.

What's the number? 42, 27, 66, 17, 81, 39

Discuss with your child any puzzles he or she makes up.

A measurement puzzle

⁶6	²1	5	■	³2	⁴1
⁵5	0	■	⁶1	7	0
0	■	⁷2	7	0	0
■	⁸7	2	■	■	■
⁹5	5	■	¹⁰1	0	5

Number chains
21, 64, 32, 16, 8, 4, 2, 1
13, 40, 20, 10, 5, 16, 8, 4, 2, 1
6, 3, 10, 5, 16, 8, 4, 2, 1
Discuss with your child the other number chains.

Factors, factors, factors Game

Which will make an open cube?
Check your child's cubes.

What angle is it? Check your child's drawings for accuracy.

Mental maths quizzes
1. 1) £5, 2)

Fraction	Decimal	Percentage
¹/₄	0·25	25%
³/₁₀	0·3	30%
¹/₅ (²/₁₀)	0·2	20%

3) Twenty-seven thousand, eight hundred and forty-five 4) 12, 24, 36, etc. 5) 750cm 6) 8000, 8300, 8320 7) £12 8) 10°C 9) 3,090 10) 36 11) –12, –6 12) 36 700 13) 570 14) a. acute, b. obtuse, c. obtuse 15) Parallel

1) £2.70, 2)

Fraction	Decimal	Percentage
$1/5$	0·2	20%
$1/4$	0·25	25%
$2/5 (4/10)$	0·4	40%

3) Eighty-three thousand, two hundred and seventeen, 4) 81, 90 or 99, 5) 2500 6) 92 000, 92 100, 92 060, 7) £45, 8) 15°C, 9) 46 200, 10) 25, 11) 2, $2^1/4$, 12) 495, 13) Decagon, 14) 338, 15) Perpendicular

3. 1) £8.37, 2)

Fraction	Decimal	Percentage
$11/20$	0·55	55%
$3/4$	0·75	75%
$1/100$	0·01	1%

3) Six hundred and five thousand, four hundred and sixteen, 4) 1, 2, 3, 4, 6, 8, 12, 24, 5) 3000, 6) 120 000, 123 000, 123 400, 123 360, 7) £70, 8) 8900, 9) 100, 10) 20, 11) 2.5, 2.75, 12) 6, 13) 3330, 14) A cube, 15) Equilateral

4. 1) £2.30, 2)

Fraction	Decimal	Percentage
$2/5$	0·4	40%
$1/100$	0·01	1%
$1/10$	0·1	10%

3) Seven hundred and twenty-five thousand, seven hundred and twenty-five, 4) 132, 5) 300, 6) 7, 9, 5, 7) £42, 8) 10, 9) –2, –4, 10) –4, 11) 14.8, 12) Tetrahedron, 13) 251, 14) Isosceles, 15) 55

5. 1) 20 weeks, 2)

Fraction	Decimal	Percentage
$4/5$	0·8	80%
$3/20$	0·15	15%
$16/100 (4/25)$	0·16	16%

3) One million, four hundred thousand, 4) 2, 4, 6, 12, 18, 36, 5) 100, 6) 200, 150, 152, 7) £36 8) 100, 9) 4·4, 5·1, 10) 22 500, 11) 170, 12) Sphere (ellipsoid or ovoid), 13) 5·2, 14) Area: 64cm², perimeter: 32cm, 15) 40 minutes

6. 1) 8, 2)

Fraction	Decimal	Percentage
$1/100$	0·01	1%
$9/20$	0·45	45%
$13/20$	0·65	65%

3) One million, seven hundred and twenty-six thousand one hundred and thirty-eight, 4) 1, 3, 5, 15, 5) 10 000, 6) 200, 240, 236, 7) £90, 8) 10, 9) –8, –12, 10) 4·5, 11) 110, 12) A cylinder, 13) 31·4, 14) 64cm, 15) 1 hour 45 minutes or 105 minutes

Maths language quizzes

Money problems: 1) 20p, 2) 12p, 3) 40p, 4) 3p, 5) 5p, 6) £1.25, 7) 90p, 8) £10, 9) £12.50, 10) £3.20

Looking at graphs: 1) Red, 2) 3, 3) 4, 4) green and yellow, 5) 37, 6) 20 kilometres, 7) 2:30, 8) They stopped (for lunch), 9) $5^1/2$ hours, 10) 11:30

Square numbers: 1) 1, 4, 9, 16, 25, 36, 49, 64, 81, 100, 2) 121, 3) 144, 4) 42, 5) 10 000, 6) 20, 7) 40, 8) 80, 9) 3rd and 4th (9 and 16), 10) 6th and 8th (36 and 64)

Decimal numbers: 1) Class 5, Class 2, Class 3, Class 4, Class 1, 2) Jack, Ranjit, Tyson, Patrick, Melanie, 3) Jack, Helen, Amy, Maria, Peter, Sunita, Bilal, George, 4) Class 1 £4, Class 2 £15, Class 3 £14, Class 4 £8, Class 5 £21, 5) Jack 6m, Melanie 4m, Tyson 4m, Patrick 4m, Ranjit 6m, 6) Amy 1.5m, Bilal 1.6m, Jack 1.5m, George 1.6m, Helen 1.5m, Maria 1.6m, Sunita 1.6m, Peter 1.6m

Fractions: 1) 15, 6, 30, 2) 15, 24, 75, 3) 60p, £3, £6, 4) 90p, £1.50, £2.70, 5) 35, 14, 70, 6) 45, 18, 90, 7) 40p, £2, £4, 8) 75p, £3.75, £7.50, 9) 30p, £1.50, £3, 36p, 60p, £1.08, 10) 60p, £3, £6, 72p, £1.20, £2.16

Area and Perimeter: 1) 6cm², 2) 14cm, 3) 11cm², 4) 16cm, 5) Area: 121mm², perimeter: 44mm, 6) Area: 225m², perimeter: 60m, 7) Area: 4000m², perimeter: 260m, 8) Area: 300m², perimeter: 74m, 9) 95cm², 10) 12cm²

Factors:

54	42	40
27	28	35
15	49	56

Percentages: 1) 50, 25, 100, 2) 10, 5, 20, 3) 20, 10, 40, 4) 8, 10, 12, 5) 4, 5, 6, 6) 16, 22, 18, 7) 24, 33, 27, 8) 75p, £1.50, £7.50, 9) 25p, 50p, £2.50, 10) 20p, 40p, £2

Number puzzles: 21, 27, 24, 42 and 60, 56, Three of 24, 48, 64, 80 and 88, 27 and 72, 248, 193, 123, 727